THE DARK RIVER

Other books by the author

A FIRST BOOK OF ANTIQUES (Heinemann)

ZOOS ARE NEWS (Abelard Schumann)

THE Dark River

by

CYRIL BRACEGIRDLE

Illustrated by
E. W. BRERETON

ALTRINCHAM
JOHN SHERRATT AND SON LTD

First Published in 1973
by
John Sherratt and Son Ltd.,
Park Road, Altrincham,
Cheshire WA14 5QQ

ISBN 0 85427 033 7

Printed in Great Britain
at the St Ann's Press, Park Road, Altrincham

To my mother
for the years of patience

FOREWORD

The modern world as we know it was born along the banks of the River Irwell in south-east Lancashire. It is a short river, a mere forty miles in length; a stream by continental standards, but its waters were used to power the looms of the first cotton mills. Shortly afterwards the power of steam was discovered and a second generation of factories rose along the river.

Britain became the workshop of the world when the machine age began by the Irwell. The story of the first river to be polluted by industry is also the story of the people who lived along that river and its tributary systems. They sailed on it for pleasure and for profit, they fished from it (before the fish died), they built bridges across it, they drowned in it, they converted part of it into the Manchester Ship Canal—and finally they nearly killed it.

If the Irwell had not existed there would still have been an Industrial Revolution—but elsewhere; and the history of Britain and of the world would have been different.

This is the life-story of a river and its people.

ACKNOWLEDGEMENTS

The author wishes to express his sincere thanks to the following persons and organizations for their kindness in supplying valuable information.

The Mersey and Weaver River Authority.

The Royal National Lifeboat Institution (Records Section).

Dr. I. M. Simpson, PH.D., F.G.S., Senior Lecturer in Stratigraphy, and Dr. F. M. Broadhurst, M.SC., PH.D., F.G.S., Senior Lecturer in Geology, both of the Department of Geology, University of Manchester.

CONTENTS

LIST OF ILLUSTRATIONS

Plates

Line Drawings

Maps

I

IN THE BEGINNING

The Irwell is all that remains of the shallow seas which covered most of south-east Lancashire about three hundred million years ago; a period known to geologists as the Upper Carboniferous when Europe lay much closer to the equator than it does today. Aeons of prehistoric time passed by unrecorded while the sea floor gradually subsided, accumulating thick deposits of mud and sand. These sediments became beds of shales and sandstones up to three hundred feet thick, alternating with sandstone and gritstone sequences of similar thickness which can be seen as extensive outcroppings on both sides of the valley that lies between the towns of Bacup and Summerseat.

The fossilized skeletons of molluscs, such as ammonioids and bivalves and other life forms, have been found, proof of this region's marine ancestry.

There are also red sandstones known as the Manchester Marles, lying in beds which are in places as much as ninety feet thick and containing numerous fossils, chiefly the imprints of the shells of molluscs.

The ice ages of the Pleistocene period, during the last one million years, have also played their part in shaping both the geology and the geography of the Irwell's course.

On several occasions the climate grew so cold that large ice sheets and glaciers formed on the upland areas of Scotland and the Lake District, spreading southwards to cover most of Lancashire. When the ice finally melted it left behind deposits of boulder clay, a dense brown clay enclosing pebbles and boulders of rocks formed millions of years earlier.

The first human settlements along the Irwell of which we have any knowledge were those of the Brigantes, a Celtic tribe, who farmed the uplands and the lower reaches of the river. In the year 79 B.C. these people must have seen a column of soldiers marching from the south with disciplined step.

On the banks of the river that ran sweet and cool between meadows of lush green grass, the soldiers eased off their breastplates and shields. In the ground before the commander's tent the standard was erected, and the setting sun gleamed on the golden eagle with which it was tipped, and on the letters SPQR (For the People and Senate of Rome).

Julius Agricola, marching up from his conquest of Anglesey and the Druids, scattering the tribes before him like leaves in the mighty wind of Roman conquest, had brought a New Order to the people of the river.

For four hundred years after his arrival the *Pax Romana* held the natives from each other's throats. The people paid their taxes and trod the surface of good Roman roads. A fortress was built at the spot where the Irwell met its tributary the Medlock, and another, smaller fortress, in an easily defended triangle formed by the Irwell, the Irk and the Hanging Ditch, this latter formation being probably a natural divide, though its origin is lost in the mists of prehistory.

Spacious villas for officers and administrators stood along the river, although their cool, shady atriums, open to the sky, were more suitable to the Mediterranean sun and too often received the drenching rains of Ultima Thule, as the conquerors called this, their farthest colony on the north-western fringes of what was then the known world.

The site of the major Roman fortress was later known as Castle Field, and an extensive archaeological dig in 1972 uncovered the remains of a civilian settlement outside the fortress. Here the natives carried out the processing of iron ore and supplied pottery and other requirements to the garrison.

As the grandeur of Rome faded and the legions withdrew to shore up the crumbling walls of empire in distant lands, so the Irwell was stained with blood and the tribes settled their differences in battle instead of in Roman courts.

Germanic invaders from the east marched along the Irwell valley, dispersing or absorbing the Celtic inhabitants. Later, chaos was replaced by the Law of the Danes as the Viking tide flowed over northern England. In A.D. 920 the Norsemen were expelled by Edward the Elder who afterwards repaired the town "that was sore defaced with the warre of the Danes".

In the Middle Ages the former Roman Mancunium grew into a large town which came to be called Manigceastre, centred within the Irwell/Irk/Hanging Ditch triangle wherein was also built a large wooden church dedicated to the English (formerly Turkish) Saint George and the French Saint Denis. This church was eventually to develop into Chetham's College.

Trading vessels plied along the river. The population increased and the city's slops were emptied into the waterway, but the Irwell could take it, cleansed as it was by the frequent rains.

In the late eighteenth century the "dark satanic mills" came, belching smoke into the once clean air, taking in raw materials and excreting their foul chemical waste into the river. Along the banks with the factories there spread the terraced hovels of the workers.

In the mid-nineteenth century a queen ascended the throne of England and across the great globe, vast areas of which were coloured red, the *Pax Britannica* held a peace that had once been held in a smaller world by the city on the Tiber.

Until the 1830s people who lived in houses near to Manchester Cathedral were still able to climb down steps cut in the red sandstone, fill flagons with water and carry it back to use for domestic purposes, even for drinking.

Edward Corbett, Borough Engineer of Salford, wrote in his book *The River Irwell* published in 1907, about "Th' owd river the memory of which lingers in old people whose courting days or other pleasant pastimes were spent on its waters or picturesque banks". Corbett also quotes his father as having told him that "About the year 1819 I have seen from the New Bailey Bridge (now called Albert Bridge) immense shoals of fish, chiefly gudgeon but other fish also were rising to the flies".

Pollutants from the expanding industries of the nineteenth century poured into the river in ever-increasing quantities. Such chemicals as gas-tar, gas-lime and ammonia water were fatal to the fish, the last of which were seen in the Irwell about 1850. In the 1860s the river was described as "almost proverbial for the foulness of its waters; receiving the refuse of cotton factories, coal mines, print works, bleach works, dye works, chemical works, paper works, almost every kind of industry".

The Victorians, to give them due credit (or some of them, anyway), were not so oblivious to the dangers of polluting the environment as we might perhaps imagine. Today, in the 1970s, scientists are giving vent to Cassandra-like wails of gloom as they picture the human race turning the earth into a giant dustbin and of mankind smothering under the weight of its own refuse; but all this was foreseen by some men more than a hundred years ago as they saw what was happening to the Irwell.

In 1867 Salford Council appointed a River Inspector whose job it was to travel the entire length, not only of the Irwell but of all its tributary streams, and to note the pollution caused by private firms and local authorities, many of whom were eventually persuaded to cease the pollution.

In 1882 Salford successfully prosecuted a firm of chemical manufacturers for pouring 3,000 tons of soda ash into the river every year. Forced to face up to the consequences of its indifference to the state of the environment the firm actually found a use for its waste which proved highly profitable, and which would probably never have been thought of had they not been compelled to do so.

Salford was able to fight so many similar actions with equally encouraging results that the condition of the Irwell began slowly to improve. In the early years of the present century it was noted that green moss and water plants, extinct for many years, were reappearing on the bed of the river.

On July 2, 1906, the Secretary of the Runcorn Anglers' Association wrote to Corbett that "The condition of the water is now nearly as good as it is possible to get it. Some of our members have put a few trout and dace in and these fish are most particular as to pure water but we have proof that they will live all right."

On September 3, 1906, the *Manchester Guardian* published the following: "The annual competition for the shield of the Worsley Canal Fishery was held at Worsley on Saturday. The catch consisted of perch, roach and eels."

What went wrong?

To find out we shall have to trace the full story of the Irwell and of the generations of the people who have lived along its banks from the time when the Industrial Revolution began.

2

SEARCH FOR THE SOURCE

The vast industrial conurbation centred on Manchester and Salford sprawls like a grey, smoky blight over the terrain of south-east Lancashire. To the north the ground rises steadily to heights of over 1,200 feet where the bleak hills attract the rain clouds sweeping in on westerly winds from the Atlantic, and it is these wet hills that nourish the Irwell and ensure its survival.

An expedition to the source of the Irwell can provide a lesson in the science of industrial archaeology. To reach the springs of history one need only journey along the A671 to the Irwell Farm, about one and a half miles to the north of Bacup. The owners of the farm are accustomed to taking visitors, from university professors, journalists and students to itinerant authors, across a muddy, gale-blasted field at the back of the farm to be shown two flat stones beneath which is a pool of dark water less than a yard in width. In the driest weather that pool is always present, still and quiet, eternally replenished by the spring that wells up from the interior of the hill.

There is a subsidary spring a few hundred yards away, but the murky pool beneath the stones is the major source.

A tiny rivulet, barely a hand-span in width, runs from the pool to trickle down hill, and a few fields away to curve round the gaunt decaying ruin of the Irwell Springs Printing Company which first opened its doors in 1813. By its side is a vast expanse of tumbled brick and stone and piled glass, the remains of another large mill that has been knocked down at some time, but nobody has bothered to remove the rubble. The air of desolation that hangs over the scene, the only noise the gurgle of the stream and the spin of a rusty ventilator in the wind, symbolizes more than anything else the overthrowing and casting down of King Cotton.

On the other side of the lane a pair of rusty iron gates bear on them in twisted iron the initials IS for Irwell Springs. The gates lead towards abandoned filter beds.

Nearby is a row of dark stone houses, still occupied. Structurally, nothing much can have changed in these parts for a hundred years or more. Long ago the "hands" would have emerged from those same houses, clogs clattering along the lane, shawls hugged tight to keep out the cold, going to work in this same factory—for many hours amid the deafening roar of the machines.

The Industrial Revolution began in these parts because of the Irwell and its numerous tributaries, and there were several reasons why the factories and mills were built here. There were so many watercourses in a comparatively small area, and the famous dampness of Lancashire was favourable to the handling of cotton. There was also perhaps an indefinable blend of talents and energies in the Lancashire character, combining with the skills of immigrant weavers from Flanders.

Irwell? The origins of the name are uncertain, but, groping through the fog of history and legend, many authorities accept the Anglo-Saxon origin: Ere-well, the "hoar or white spring". These rolling hills which gave it birth bear the name of Deerplay Moor, also of Anglo-Saxon derivation, meaning Deer-Uplay, the upland vale of the deer.

If the Irwell had never spouted here, flowing from the vale of the upland deer down to the Mersey, the Industrial Revolution would still have happened, but not here. Along some other system of waterways the wheels of the machine age would have spun.

The water of the stream is tainted with iron-oxide deposits from ancient coal mines, the Old Deerplay and Old Meadows Mines. The latter was one of Britain's most unusual collieries, of interest both to geologists and to industrial archaeologists for the way in which the main coal seam, the Union Mine, can be seen to split into two thinner but separate seams, called the Lower Mountain and the Upper Foot Mines respectively, when traced through the colliery workings.

The coal was worked by the pillar-and-stall method. It was hand-loaded into tubs which were hauled along a narrow-gauge railway by an endless chain system straight out of the pit, across the fields and into Bacup.

When this colliery was closed in 1969 strenuous but unsuccessful efforts were made by interested parties to have it preserved as a museum of coal mining and geology.

Coal was not the only natural product in these regions which man found very useful; there was also the sandstone known to geologists as the Millstone Grit Series. These massively bedded gritty sandstones, such as the Rough Rock which crops out on the flanks of Harcles Hill high above Holcombe, farther downstream, and high on Scout Moor above Edenfield, provided the source for a major industry in the valley for centuries. Just underneath the Rough Rock can be found the Haslingden Flags, a group of thinly bedded, very hard, fine-grained quartzite sand-stones. Many thousands of paving stones have been quarried from these beds to line the streets of towns and villages throughout Britain.

Nature has provided not only coal and flags here, but the Deerplay Fault as well. On March 7, 1972, at 6.55 a.m., deep in the earth below the Moor and the ever-seeping springs that feed the Irwell, rocks that are infinitely older than the race of man moved slightly against each other.

In Bacup a chimney came crashing into the street. Crockery collected for an Easter Fair at Burgess Becker Junior School, Harpurhey, in Manchester, was smashed to pieces. In the small towns of Leyland, Accrington, Walton-le-Dale, Rawtenstall and Heywood, people awoke with alarm to find their ceilings suddenly cracking. As far away as Astbury near Congleton in Cheshire, houses trembled. The whole incident lasted for ten seconds and was registered at Eskdalemuir Observatory in Dumfriesshire as a weak tremor.

The Deerplay Fault had moved again.

The British Isles, well away from the major earthquake zones that girdle the earth, are not accustomed to such happenings, but even here, in these relatively safe latitudes, there are "faults" which from time to time cause minor tremors.

The main fault in Lancashire is the Irwell Valley Fault itself which can be traced for more than ten miles laterally and has a maximum displacement of the strata of more than one thousand yards. The northwest-southwest trend of the valley between Bolton and Salford is guided by this fault line.

The local press invariably ascribe all tremors to the Pendleton Fault, but geologists regard this as only a branch of the main Irwell Valley Fault which is responsible for most of the tremors. The Deerplay Fault is another major fault running parallel to that of the Irwell Valley.

Major tremors from one or other of the faults were recorded in February 1899, April 1900 and in November 1905, all causing some damage to property in the Salford area. There were tremors in Bacup in September 1777 and in March 1869, which seem to have resulted in much alarm at the time. In between these dates there have been numerous minor vibrations.

Around the source of the Irwell the hills are littered with wrecked and abandoned mills, each surrounded by its dumps of industrial waste. A thousand broken windows look out on the man-blasted heaths. Cotton had its hour here and then died and, in these Hills of the Beginning nothing has come to replace it. The desolate mills are like ancient forts where a revolution began and then swept on down the valley, leaving them behind. The ordnance survey map is studded with tanks, springs, cloughs, weirs and air shafts to old mine workings.

A poet of long ago wrote of this region:

> Behold, behold, with wondrous eyes
> The towering hills that reach the skies,
> The fertile plain and vale below
> Where the lovely streams of Irwell flow.

But that was before the chimneys blackened the trees, so that even the native moths had to breed a darker strain because the lighter-coloured ones stood out against the black foliage and so were picked off by their enemies, natural selection responding to man's pollution of the environment.

Leaving Deerplay Moor, it is possible to follow the Irwell downhill towards Bacup. Held tightly between concrete walls, the river is about two yards wide as it flows by the side of the A671 into the town.

Modern bungalows, interspersed among the older stone houses lining the road in traditional ribbon developement, indicate that not everyone dislikes this region of scrubby grass and ruined mills and strong winds.

In Bacup there are long rows of terraced houses made

of dark grey local stone; though these days many have modernized doors and windows, indicating a society which has become more affluent than in the days of cotton as commuter communications have linked the inhabitants with other industrial centres.

From Bacup to Rawtenstall, a distance of about five miles, the towns of Bacup, Nun Hills, Stacksteads, Hugh Mill, Waterfoot, Clough Fold and Rawtenstall all run into each other without much distinction—a linear conurbation linked by the A681.

The Irwell now begins to greet its satellite streams. At Stacksteads it is joined by several small brooks flowing from both north and south. Near Waterfoot the Whitwell Brook comes in from the north side and from the south the Cowpe Brook dances in.

The brook known as Limey Water follows a wayward, indecisive course down through the Forest of Rossendale whose trees mostly vanished a long time ago, and merges with the Irwell at Rawtenstall. From here the river curves south-west, still following the A681, until just south of Ewood Bridge where it meets the River Ogden, itself a continuation of the Swinnel Brook.

Between Rawtenstall and Ramsbottom it is possible to see, standing out on Holcombe Moor, the huge tower erected to the memory of the Peel family who dominated this region in the age of cotton. A staircase leads to the upper gallery from which, over 500 feet above the valley, one can look north towards Pendle and the country of the Lancashire witches written about by Harrison Ainsworth.

Opposite Peel Tower, on the other side of the valley, is the Grant Tower, dedicated to William and Daniel Grant, two brothers whose "energy, perseverance, prudent thrift with generous benevolence and hospitality" were renowned, so much so that they were acknowledged by Dickens as being the originals of the Cheeryble Brothers in *Nicholas Nickleby*.

The Irwell now runs south until Radcliffe is reached, by which time it has absorbed and been strengthened by Holcombe Brook and Kirklees Brook (known as Tottington Brook in its earlier stages).

At Radcliffe the River Roch adds its quota. The writer Edwin Waugh, who knew it in its more youthful days, seems to have had a liking for this river, for in 1889 he wrote:

Oh, gentle Roch, my native stream,
   Oft when a careless boy,
I've prattled to thee, in a dream,
   As thou went singing by.

Like thee, my little life glides down,
   To the great absorbing main,
From whose mysterious dens unknown,
   We ne'er return again.

After Radcliffe the Irwell's course is due west, taking in Croal Major at Prestolee. Croal Major is a mixture of Croal Minor, the Tonge River and Bradshaw Brook. Now we are nearing the great conurbation itself, habitation of about two million people, who are here in skyscraper flats, houses, offices, factories, shopping precincts, power stations, because, aeons ago, a spring began to gush forth on the vale of the deer.

The Irwell glides on, through Carr Clough, past the racecourse, to its meeting with the grimy Irk at Hunts Bank where Agricola's legion built its fort, past the Cathedral, cleaned now and resplendent on a sunny day, under Victoria Bridge, past the ghost of Pomona Gardens and on to its final marriage with the Manchester Ship Canal.

3

RAGING TORRENTS

For the Irwell to flood over its banks today is a rare event and a very minor sort of flood indeed. Many dams and weirs control its course, taming and confining a river once wild and free. In former days the Irwell often wreaked immense damage to the humans who dared to hem its way with bricks and concrete.

Under the influence of abnormal rains the river would gather strength in the high lands above Bacup, swell with the contents of the laden clouds sweeping in from the Atlantic, and hurl itself downstream towards Manchester and Salford.

Earlier records, back to 1616, mention a day on which the Irwell rose "to heights never known. It is an easy matter with God to drowne a towne, yea, even a world".

A survey made in 1800 commented:

> Along the Irwell and its tributary streams above the town of Manchester, there are 400 mills and other

> manufacturing establishments all of which have reservoirs great and small. In winter, floods are frequent on the rivers (sometimes there are three or four in a week) and when these happen in daytime the hands, who have no employment in the mills during their continuance, must either retrieve lost time or lose their wages.

One of the worst and best documented of such disasters was the great flood of 1866. On a day in November the river threw its fury upon a people who already knew hardship enough. Work and bed was their world. Work and bed, breathing in the smoke-polluted air by day and the disease-ridden odours of the river by night. They were to know more suffering still when the river, grown suddenly to a giant in the pouring rains of a westerly storm, surged against its imprisoning walls. Tree trunks and other debris—even rocks—were borne on its furious tide. In the hills a thousand streams flashed into existence and fed the Irwell—fed it so that it became a ravening, pounding, thundering monster.

Soon factories were awash. In Radcliffe the filthy water swirled around the looms, probing into the engine-rooms where great clouds of steam hissed angrily as the irresistible force sizzled against the hot sides of the boilers—and then cataracted on to the fires themselves.

In the fetid riverside slums of Manchester and Salford many families lived in cellar rooms. The first they knew of danger was when the water poured down through already broken windows on to their heads, and where

A scene from the great flood of 1866

C

the windows were intact the invader flowed down the cellar steps.

Louis M. Hayes, in his *Reminiscences of Manchester,* which was published in 1905, gives this account of the flood:

> On the 17th of November, a great and disastrous flood occurred which caused widespread and terrible damage to property. From the present racecourse at the Cliff right away to the Crescent, Salford, there extended a huge lake of turbid water, rushing irresistibly along, carrying in its course everything which it was capable of uprooting.
>
> It was a truly magnificent sight to those who could from some point of safety stand and take in the panorama of seething waters which lay stretched out before them. But to those who had life and property at stake it was a day of disaster and never-ceasing anxiety and dread.
>
> In Broughton Lane, and in many other places, the inhabitants might be seen sailing about from house to house in boats or on rafts, and, in fact, upon anything that would float and carry them to some place of safety.
>
> In many dwellings the water was not only in the cellars and in the living rooms, but it might be seen rising up into the bedrooms. Hundreds of families were crowded together in the attics and upper rooms of their houses and cottages, looking with alarm at the water as it mounted higher and higher, lapping against the

stairs and cutting off any retreat from their watery prison.

It was a serious and anxious sight by the afternoon to watch the rapid swirl of muddy brown water as it came shooting along past you, and carrying away on its angry-looking bosom all manner of incongruous things.

Imagine seeing a dead pig, a family group of cocks and hens perched disconsolately on an old hencoop, in company with a host of miscellaneous articles of all shapes and sizes; household and otherwise; dog-kennels, trees, bandboxes, furniture of all descriptions, hats, wooden boxes and floating crockery, all rushing wildly along and at times jostling and falling foul of one another, as if they were hurrying on and away from some relentless foe who was driving them to destruction, and from whom they were powerless to escape.

In Strangeways the water lay deep in the roadway, and passengers in the omnibuses at places had to put their feet on the opposite seats, to try and keep clear of the water which came lapping in as we drove along.

I saw one courageous cabman driving along with his fare inside, attempt to breast the full force of the flood as he entered Broughton Lane, but he had not proceeded far before the depth of the water forced him to turn round and beat a hasty retreat, as had he not quickly done so the consequences might have been serious.

The sight presented next morning was truly pitiable;

the furniture and household belongings in hundreds of dwellings were hopelessly damaged or destroyed; the trees which lay in the course of the flood looked as if they had been fishing on their own account and had had a good haul in the shape of straw, rags, paper, old baskets, etc., in fact anything appeared to be fish which came to their net by finding a lodgment in their branches.

In the aftermath the disaster was reported at length in the *Free-Lance,* a humorous magazine of the time, by an unknown journalist making use of some rather heavy-witted flights of fancy and sprinkling his copy with those classical allusions which were so beloved of Victorian writers.

Last week every brook became a river, every rill a torrent, every pond a whirlpool; cellars were flooded, works inundated, machinery spoiled; numbers of workers thereby deprived of occupations; as a consequence the poor rates are increased and the Manchester public has to pay through its nasal ornament for results which ought to be avoided by the owners of property on the banks of the river.

The damage done to the pretty borders in Peel Park was tremendous. A lovely promenade has been covered with mud; defunct dogs and departed cats are to be found where erst the dahlia and the aster reflected the rays of Phoebus; seats overturned, borders demolished.

Whoever is to pay for the work necessary to prevent this periodic visitation—whether the ratepayers at large or the property owners in particular—let it be done at once. That the city should remain in perpetual fear of these inundations is a scandal to its management and a disgrace to the Aldermen and Councillors of Manchester and Salford.

On October 22 of the following year a further comment appeared in the *Free-Lance* :

Our excellent River Irwell has made several demonstrations during the last few days. This usually sluggish but convenient old sewer takes its pernicious and meandering course through the city and borough, easily and slowly, at its own definitely indolent "sweet" will.

Hundreds and thousands of the "industrial orders" who live in a state of local anarchy along its miles of factory-laden banks, fling their little mountains of pestiferous ordure into a stream naturally inoffensive and salubrious. By the time the poor outraged river, bearing in its veins its burthen of abominations, is able to shew itself to the Corporations of Manchester and Salford, it is in an evil plight indeed. It then slackens its course, as it were, and pauses to appeal for a little "municipal pity".

Did you ever see, Messieurs of the Town Halls, such a poor, blackened, suffocated, poisoned, demoralised, monstrous piece of river misery since you were severally born of your respected mothers?" the Irwell seems to mutter. "Have you, since your earliest baptismal moments, beheld such a barbarian spectacle as I am? Barbarian did I say? The broad sweet innocent stream in which the savage of the far wilderness laves his brown limbs and in which his un-panniered bride can see his own wild loveliness, is purity itself in comparison with me, a part of the fine civilisation of nature."

Poor, horrid old hag of the river-world, thy wail will avail thee nothing. "It is true," the dismal creature might go on in its beseeching, despairing way, "It is true that you cannot altogether ignore the great wrongs I suffer, because, generally speaking, and in the speech of the vulgar, you know a trick worth two of that. You go to live in suburban palladian villas where my soothing exhalations cannot reach you, and you come down of a morning, per bus or rail, or in your own natty little drags, looking smug and ruddy, and thankful to a benign providence which kindly watches over the sweet little cherubs that sit up aloft in municipal committee rooms and who are not as other men.

"Oh, yes; amongst the multifarious businessmen which attract your salubrious and highly-wasted attention—such as looking after your own flesh and blood when there are any desirable little contracts about; such as profitable gas-tar dealings, which don't bear analysis, chemical or conscientious; such as stultifying yourselves about me; such as never knowing your own mind (when you rise to the abnormal condition of having one); such as taking two years' service as Mayor out of one of the few men who are an honour to you, asking him to give you another year gratis, and, snobbishly, and in ruffianly way, insulting him when you did it; such as, amidst all this kind of public-spirited behaviour; gentlemen, you certainly find time for a considerable stroke of business in the way of whited sepulchres.

"The people I poison are not you, ye meek and mild; it is the tiny ones in their mothers' arms, who haven't yet acquired the strength to toddle, and never will! It is the ghastly young mothers who cry their foolish eyes out when their little ones are cold and still, and have given over being troublesome and lie white in the small cradle that comes from the cheap undertaker. It is such as these that I kill, because, unlike the smug and ruddy committee men—they can't get away from my invaluable company."

Why do we descant so amply about the recent floods instead of discoursing on municipal affairs? Ungentle reader, the Irwell is a municipal affair. The wide and preventable destruction of property by such floods is a municipal affair. The poisoning of small children is a municipal affair. Shall we, unenlightened and too matter-of-fact people of the city or borough, label for these everything which it is the business and duty of the Corporation to do or to leave undone as the American artist labelled his picture, and chalk upon it for thy instructions the words "This is Municipal Business"? Suffice it to say that the Irwell matter is a representative question. In it we can discern for some

> considerable degree the flagrant failure of municipal government. We see in it the chartered incorporation of vanity, of cynicism, of corruption, of snobbery, of recklessness of life and property, and of boundless ruffianly shamelessness with which our two corporations are so dismally "sickled o'er".

It is an interesting point that, with all this cumbersome style of writing the journalist of those days was able to accuse the authorities of corruption and double dealing, of being snobs and ruffians, of indulging in "desirable little contracts . . . which don't bear analysis". For such writing today the journalist would find himself in court accused of libel—if his editor were so foolish as to let his words appear in print at all. We pride ourselves on our vaunted freedom of speech, yet we are no longer able to call one of our lords and masters a scoundrel.

During the morning after one particular flood in 1866, the crowds gathered in front of Manchester Cathedral and watched furniture, trees, barrels, dead livestock floating by. The owners of a timber yard opposite the Cathedral had to witness the sight of their entire stock floating away, despite strenuous efforts made to restrain it.

The Palatine Bridge was at one time four feet under water and in the Strangeways area many families were marooned in their homes. Pleasure boats were brought from Belle Vue to help in the rescue work. One quite large boat was found high and dry in the forecourt of number 50, Bury New Road.

In the Broughton district, rescue parties led by the Mayor, working with frenzied zeal, succeeded in delivering 700 people from their flooded homes to the safety of the Town Hall, the Workhouse, the Gas Offices and St. John's Catholic School. A man who tried to make his way across Duke Street, opposite Grosvenor Terrace, lost his footing, was swept away and drowned.

The great flood of 1866 was the worst ever recorded, but there were bad floods in even earlier times. The flood of 1799 is mentioned in the well-known novel *The Manchester Man* (1876 by Mrs Linnæus Banks, of whom E. L. Burney wrote an interesting biography in 1969). Mrs. Banks, obviously drawing on ancient records for her descriptive material, wrote:

> The tannery yard, high as it was above the bed of the Irk, and solid as was its embankment, was threatened with invasion. The surging water roared and beat against its masonry, and licked its coping with frothy tongue and lip, like a hungry giant, greedy for fresh food.
>
> Men with thick cloths and hide-bound legs, leather gloves and aprons, were hurrying to and fro with barrows and bark-boxes for the reception of the valuable hides which their mates, armed with long-shafted hooks and tongs, were dragging from the pits pell-mell, ere the advancing waters should encroach upon their territory, and empty the tan-pits for them.

The Irwell was never a Ganges or a raging Mississippi;

but looking at the dark, oily, turgid stream oozing slowly between the walls of warehouses and factories today, it is difficult to imagine that this river has many times caused so much havoc.

4

THE BRIDGES OF THE IRWELL

The first bridge across the Irwell was almost certainly a wooden one near the present Victoria Bridge, later replaced by a stone structure built in 1368 when Thomas del Bothe, a wealthy journeyman, left the sum of £30 in his will towards the cost of a bridge.

When finally built this had three arches and was wide enough for one cart. Every few yards there was a recess into which a pedestrian could step for safety when a cart passed. Half-way across was a small chapel wherein travellers leaving Manigceastre invariably paused to offer a prayer for a safe journey and another of thanksgiving if they returned without harm.

The old bridge, however, experienced many changes. The time came when the chapel, associated with today's Chapel Street on the Salford side, fell into disuse and of its two rooms the lower one became a prison. Nothing was likely to sober a drunken man more quickly than a night spent in that cold damp dungeon fighting the huge colony of ever-hungry rats that had their permanent home there almost at water level.

Many very badly bitten prisoners emerged the next morning to be fined the sum of sixpence. If they were unable to pay, the money was collected from the landlord who had supplied the liquor on the previous night, a procedure which might be difficult to impose upon the modern publican. The prisoners also had to face the dangers of the dungeon being flooded, and there is a record of at least one unfortunate individual having been drowned when heavy rains caused the river to rise rapidly during the night. The chapel was finally removed when the bridge was widened in 1775.

During the Civil War the bridge proved to be a decisive military factor in saving Manchester for the Parliamentary forces. When the conflict between King and Parliament began in 1642 it found Salford on one side of the Irwell favouring the monarchist cause while Manchester on the other side was at first fairly evenly divided. After some weeks of argument the Parliamentary party gained the ascendancy and the two cities faced each other in argumentative mood across the narrow water.

Only verbal missiles were exchanged, but in mid-September alarming news came that a royalist force under Lord Strange was assembling at Warrington for a march on Manchester.

A defence committee was formed and a resident German engineer, who apparently knew all about siege works and similar military activity, was engaged to supervise the setting up of various defences, despite the mutterings of the city's royalist minority and threats to sabotage the defences.

On September 24 the main royalist force appeared on the Salford bank. Two men were sent out from Manchester to enquire, as an anonymous eyewitness afterwards wrote, "Of the meaning of their coming in so hostile a manner".

This façade of innocence by the Mancunians cut little ice with Lord Strange who proved himself to be no gentleman by seizing one of the messengers as hostage and returning the other in company with a Captain Windebank to demand entrance to the city. If such entrance were granted he promised to treat the inhabitants gently; if not, Captain Windebank spoke gloomily of "fearful destruction ensuing".

Undaunted, the gallant Mancunians looked to their defences. At noon the invaders began to "play with cannon upon Deansgate and Salford Bridge", those royalist Salfordians having allowed free use of their side of the river.

The Mancunians defended their territory but at first were "beaten back because the wind blew smoke and flame into our faces". The anonymous eyewitness seems to have been of a poetic turn of mind for he goes on, "But God who rides upon the wings of the wind, suddenly turned it till the rage of the fire was abated".

Having the deity on one's side has always been an advantage in warfare, even though the opposition tend to regard it as somewhat unfair; and with God's aid the defenders drove the royalists back on to the Salford bank where they entrenched themselves in a house at the base of the bridge and continued firing throughout the night.

For a whole week the battle swayed to and fro, and then the royalists, having lost 200 killed, retreated back to Warrington, and Manchester was saved for Parliament. An eyewitness expresses great astonishment, as well he might, that the defender's total casualties were two men killed and two wounded. One of the fatalities was not a fighter at all but a weaver named Richard Perceaval, a lad who managed to get his name in the history books because he sat on a stile near to the churchyard in order to view the fighting and had the misfortune to be struck by a stray bullet—which proves that wars are safer watched from a distance.

The royalist forces had mustered 4,000 foot with seven pieces of ordnance, 100 horsemen and 204 dragoons. A dragoon was a horseman using a flint-lock pistol which made such a noise, spitting smoke and fire, that the riders came to be known as dragons, later lengthened to dragoons.

It was calculated that during the entire week the royalists fired a total of more than 4,000 bullets, out of which by some freakish chance they apparently succeeded in hitting four of the heroic and fast-moving—except for the unlucky Richard Perceaval—defenders of Manchester.

The Hanging Ditch also had a bridge, built in the early part of the fifteenth century. It may well have been a drawbridge and one theory is that the name Hanging Ditch implies that the bridge was "hung" in the air. The

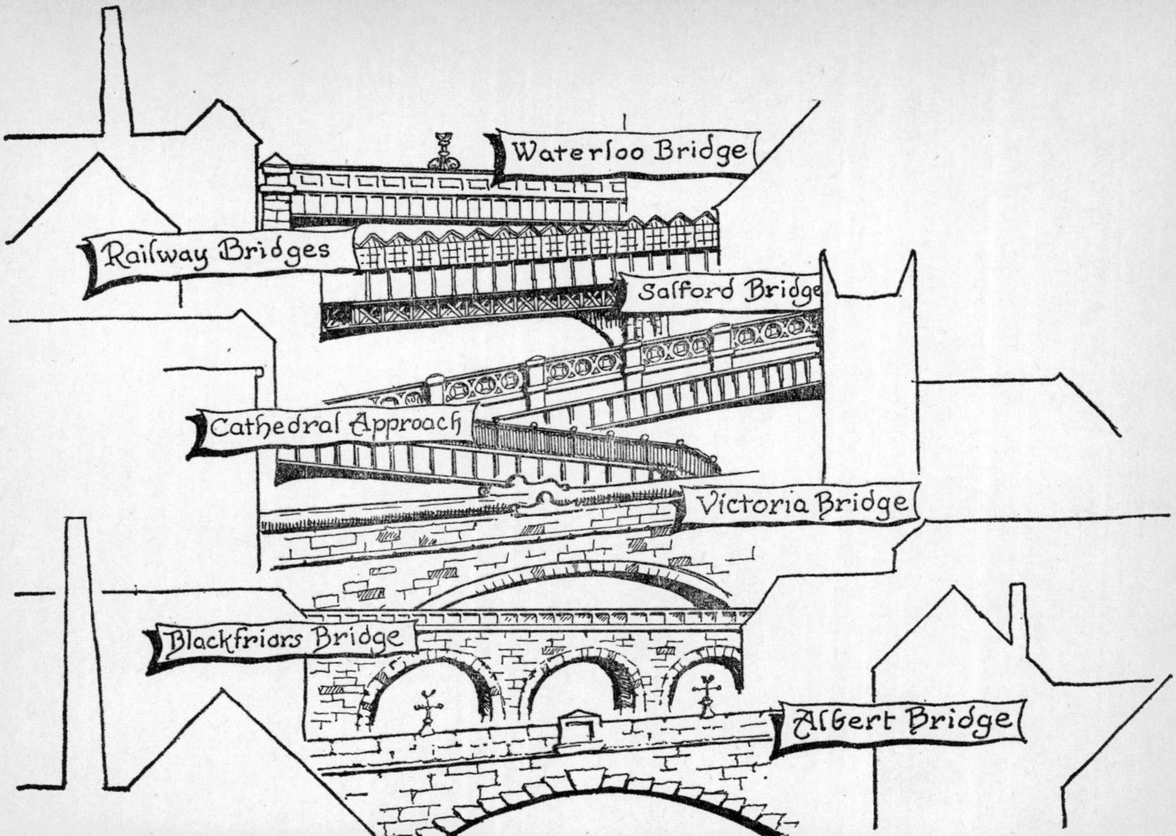
Waterloo Bridge
Railway Bridges
Salford Bridge
Cathedral Approach
Victoria Bridge
Blackfriars Bridge
Albert Bridge

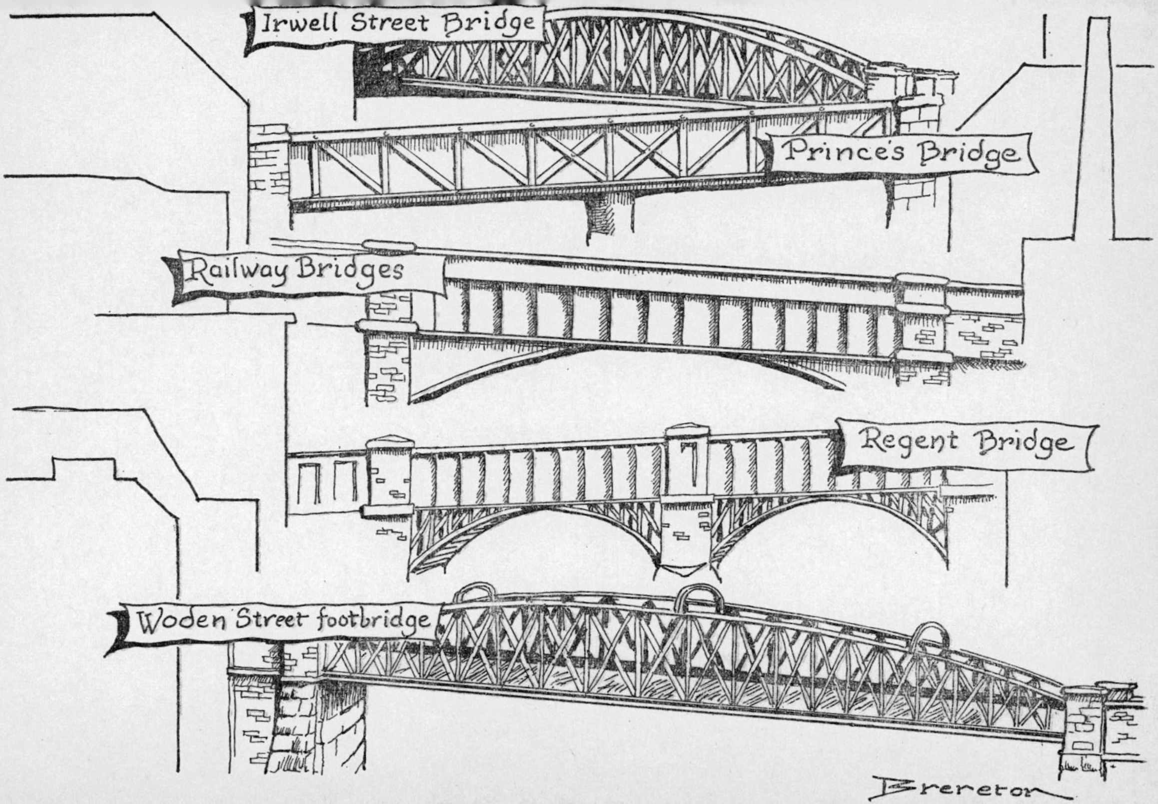

Bridges linking Manchester and Salfard

name is also similar to the Saxon "hengen" meaning hill, though it is difficult to see how this could relate to a ditch. Yet another theory about the name is that prisoners were led over the bridge to a place of execution at the Cateaton end. Origins are so lost in the mist of centuries that one guess is as good as another.

The bridge itself was of wood supported on stone buttresses, and in 1881 excavations for new buildings revealed these supports which had been lost to sight when the great ditch was filled in.

Richard Wright Proctor, in his book *Memorials of Bygone Manchester,* described a walk across the new Victoria Bridge in 1879:

> The bridge was thronged with traffic including groups of street-singers warbling with due plaintiveness *Home Sweet Home,* a melody then just composed and which seemed to possess a peculiar charm. Scarcely had we parted from the wandering minstrels and reached the centre or neutral ground of the bridge when our attention was arrested by the novel cry of "Hot Chelsea Buns" and one of the steaming tempters was soon placed at our disposal by a peripatetic vendor who was that well-known and kindly-remembered baker who lived and traded during a long series of years in Salford. There he commanded and baked those delicious morsels contrived originally at the Old Bun House in Chelsea. For an entire generation from 1823 this Chelsea bun man was a trader of mark and interest in our midst.

The bun man's regular round was to enter Manchester from the Salford side of the river via the Blackfriars Bridge and to return over Victoria Bridge. It is the former construction which often arouses the most comment from amateur historians who wonder if there was actually a "black friar". There was indeed a company of the Black Friars established in Pendleton in 1898, but as the present bridge was opened and named in 1820 a connection cannot be established. The name may have originated with a much earlier bridge thrown across the same place in 1761. This was little more than a wooden footbridge and was paid for and constructed by, of all things, a theatrical company! The company performed at a riding school in Salford and wanted better access for their patrons on the Manchester side. Accordingly they built the bridge and named it, so the story goes, after the Blackfriars Bridge then being built in London and which did apparently take its name from a London Dominican community.

An unknown poet of the time has left us these lines:

In the year seventeen sixty and sixty-one,
The town by the players was well played upon,
Old Whitley* possession had got of the town,
But two London Houses† joined forces and came down,
And no place being vacant that was near to the centre,
They determined in Salford to try their adventure,
Erected a building, erected a stage,

* Old Whitley was the owner of the theatre.
† Covent Garden and Drury Lane Theatres.

to act o'er the passions of man and the age,
and to tempt the Manchestrians made steps down the
ridge,
And over the river threw Blackfrairs Bridge.

One of the men working on the later stone bridge must have wanted to leave something for posterity. He buried in the brickwork a cricket ball and a bottle made of thick green glass marked "Townsend's Aerated Waters, Salford". These items were found by a bricklayer in 1970 when some work was being done on the bridge as part of the construction of a stairway from Blackfriars Street down to a car park at river level.

In the late nineteenth century the inhabitants of Manchester and Salford were under no illusions about the quality of the river that divided the two cities, for when the Suez Canal was open in 1869 the Irwell was jokingly dubbed the "Sewage Canal"! In that same year as the celebrations in Egypt a minor event took place for which Verdi was *not* commissioned to write an opera; if he had it would have had to be a comic opera to mark the opening of a footbridge across the Irwell.

The event was described by a correspondent on the *Free-Lance*:

> To be forewarned is to be forearmed—so saith the proverb, but there are people who will not be warned, and who consequently come to grief. Of such are the Mayor of Salford, Mr. Cawley, C.E. and M.P. for that ancient borough, Mr Newton, another C.E. and the committee for building the new foot bridge between

Broughton and Peel Park. It would be unkind in the extreme to impute, either to the Mayor or any of the parties concerned, that they do not diligently peruse the pages of the *Free-Lance,* and yet how little they heed its warnings! The Mayor actually had a copy of last week's issue sticking out of his side pocket, and that identical number contained this ominous line:

"A subject not to be dipped into—The Irwell",

and yet, nevertheless, not withstanding, the Mayor and his party actually did the very thing they were cautioned not to do: they dipped into the Irwell, and we hope they liked it.

The manner of the dip was as follows: Assembled on a platform were the Mayor, in his collar, Mr. Cawley, holding a trowel in one hand and a mallet in the other, Mr. Crossland, who was going to spread mortar on a coping stone, tap it with the mallet, and declare it to be "well and truly laid", young Mr. Buxton, who carried an address elegantly written, and still more elegantly framed.

The sun was darting its post-meridian rays full upon the heads of the people, and there arose from the Irwell the smell of many species of defunct fish, and the odour of sundry sewers and cesspools. To the nostrils of the natives of the banks, these sweet perfumes were grateful and refreshing—they told of science and of civilisation, of immunity from taxes, of cholera and typhus.

Three medical men and two undertakers were observed to be especially buoyant and jovial, but still the Irwell looked like a thing not to be dipped into.

"Ladies and gentlemen", said the Mayor, "we are assembled upon this auspicious occasion to take an active, I may say an important part, in the erection of a structure which—is to bind the inhabitants of Broughton and—and Salford in bonds of closer union. It is a token of amity and friendship. Before its approval will—will disappear—!"

What more the Mayor would have said, who can tell, for at that critical moment he himself disappeared below the flooring of the stage on which he was declaiming. And not only his worship, but the M.P. with the mallet and trowel, and a host of fine ladies in their ruffs and crinolines. The platform did not exactly break down, it merely, out of fun, assumed an angle of 75 degrees, and shot its occupants into the river. Some of the newspapers say that the Mayor and the M.P. did not go into the water. We know better. Why, was not Mr. Cawley seen with just his chin above mud—scarcely fair to say water—holding aloft the trowel and the mallet with which he had been entrusted by the committee? Was not the Mayor observed to puff and blow with distress as the semi-liquid stream reached his vitals, and deranged his stomach? Very well then.

As to Mr. Crossland he somehow "hung on", and was immediately smothered beneath the voluminous crinoline and borne down by the substantial—well—legs—why not?—of a lady of sixteen stone, more or less, who alighted upon his shoulders, and whose boots expressed with a desirable emphasis a desire to be "taken off". The address which was to have been presented to the worthy stone-layer concealed itself in the Irwell's bed, thus showing a degree of impudence —not to say immodesty, which would never have been exposed if it had reached its proper destination. Two ladies, waving white and blue parasols, were stuck in the mud about two yards from the shore, and shrieked hysterically as a good natured but thoughtless gentleman on the bank began to denude himself of his apparel preparatory to plunging—no, squashing—in to their rescue. As they took short and cautious steps towards safety, they screamed anew as they became conscious of the stuff into which they had so thoughtlessly dipped, and which, at each successive advance insinuated itself more copiously beneath their—socks.

Numerous articles found in the river after the accident have been left at our office, and await identification, viz.: seventeen chignons, including three of a reddish tint, a hood with a portrait of a butcher; three shoes, numbers 4, 3½, and 5 all for the left foot; a letter, adressed to "My darling Jemmy"; two and a half pairs of moustaches; three auburn curls, two front teeth, and five molars; two blue stockings, and last of all the very address which was taken out of the bed of the Irwell at 2 a.m. on Sunday morning, by the intelligent officer, X. Y. Z. No. 99, by him duly conveyed to Corporation Street, and which we shall have the greatest pleasure in presenting to Mr. Crossland, if he will call at anytime before 7 a.m., or after 11 p.m. supposing he should be at home at the time.

Mr. Johnson, the contractor, who, it must be supposed, had the erection of the platform which acted so well upon the occasion, is a benefactor to his race, and deserves a statue. He has indirectly caused the Mayor and Civil Engineers to taste of the water of the Irwell, and to prove that in its present state it ought, certainly, not to be dipped into. Probably this accident may lead to a cleansing of the river, and if so, why, then, a statue for Johnson, by all means.

As no loss of life has occurred we can now laugh at the event. But if the other M.P. for Salford had been present he must, most assuredly, have been suffocated, for no man of four-feet-one can hope to dip into the Irwell, and live. How sad to reflect that but for Mr. Charley's fortunate absence, the first man upon whom the new Coroner of Salford would have sat, would have been the M.P. for the Borough.

As population increased over both banks the Irwell was spanned by more and more bridges. There was the chain bridge in Lower Broughton which crashed into the river in 1831 when a company of the 60th Rifle Corps foolishly attempted to cross it marching in step—fortunately there were no casualties, but a curious coincidence was that the bridge had been built by the father-in-law of the officer in command.

There was once a wooden tubular bridge, entirely roofed in, which led to Castle Irwell. In the flood of 1866 it was washed from its supports. Great crowds watched it float down river, expecting it to smash into the Gerald Road Bridge, but it touched and rolled over, finally coming to rest at the Crescent in Salford.

There is a stretch of the river along which it is possible to take quite a pleasant walk even today. This begins just behind the angular blocks of Salford University where a broad riverside walk winds by the side of Peel Park and passes a new bridge, a graceful concrete span which gives access to the Civil Engineering building of the University on the far side.

It is easy to imagine what a superb riverside walk this could be, especially if continued farther back round the curve of the Crescent. The Irwell Promenade would make a fine Sunday afternoon stroll. All that it needs is some initiative—and a little money.

The river here is about 35 yards wide, and the walk continues for perhaps 500 yards to Frederick Road Bridge beyond which one cannot pass. This bridge, a substantial structure formerly called Wallness Bridge, cost £26,515 and was opened on May 1, 1880, by the Mayor of Salford.

Close to Frederick Road there is a footbridge known by the picturesque name of Rivers Dale after the street which gives access to it. In May 1972 people using this bridge were surprised to see several wild ducks swimming placidly on the murky water below. One even had a small family of four chicks plodding along in its wake. They had left an ornamental—and quite clean—pond in a nearby park, possibly after some domestic tiff with the other inhabitants, and had chosen to set up home on the Irwell, even, in one case, to breed on it. An indication, perhaps, that the river in this area has been improved to the extent that it is now only dirty as distinct from being poisonous.

5

STATELY HOMES

The Radcliffe family arrived on the Irwell during the fourteenth century when Sir John Radcliffe, a Norman knight who had fought at Crécy, built himself a house on the banks of the river. Over the years the house developed into a black-and-white timbered structure and became known as Ordsall Hall, from the much older Saxon name of Woerdesael.

A tree-lined lane led from the house into the village of Salford—a village which Sir John transformed into a thriving centre of commerce. It is he who is credited with having brought to the region those Flemish weavers who in later years helped to create the cotton industry.

Sir John died of the plague in 1362, having in his time also held the Manor of Moston which passed to Henry de Strangeways in 1394.

After the upheaval of the Reformation the Radcliffes remained staunch to the Catholic faith, but they were also a practical family who preferred to try to preserve their lands and keep their heads off the block. Consequently, in Elizabethan times, while continuing to observe the ritual of Rome, they also swore undying loyalty to the Queen. They regularly paid the fines imposed upon local Catholics who continued to follow their faith, and another John, who lived in the Elizabethan period, was more than once accused of being a "dangerous temporiser".

When, in 1564, the Catholics rose in revolt on behalf of Mary, Queen of Scots, they looked to Sir John for support, but the Radcliffes, knowing how to survive in troubled times, raised a company of loyalists at Ordsall and rode to join the Earl of Essex at York where he was preparing to crush the revolt.

In 1571 Sir John was appointed Knight of the Shire and in 1574 he joined the Association of Lancashire Gentlemen formed to defend the Queen from the conspirators who supported the so-called Queen of Scots.

During the Civil War the Radcliffes supported the Royalist cause. They welcomed at Ordsall Lords Strange and Molyneux who stayed there overnight on their unsuccessful march to seize Manchester for the King.

Sir Alexander Radcliffe, head of the family at that time, was wounded at the battle of Edge Hill. During the Commonwealth he was imprisoned in the Tower for a while and on being released he returned to Ordsall, where he died in 1654.

The Civil War depleted the Radcliffes' fortune considerably and after the death of Sir Alexander they could no longer afford the upkeep of the hall. It was sold in 1662 to Colonel John Birch, a rich Puritan.

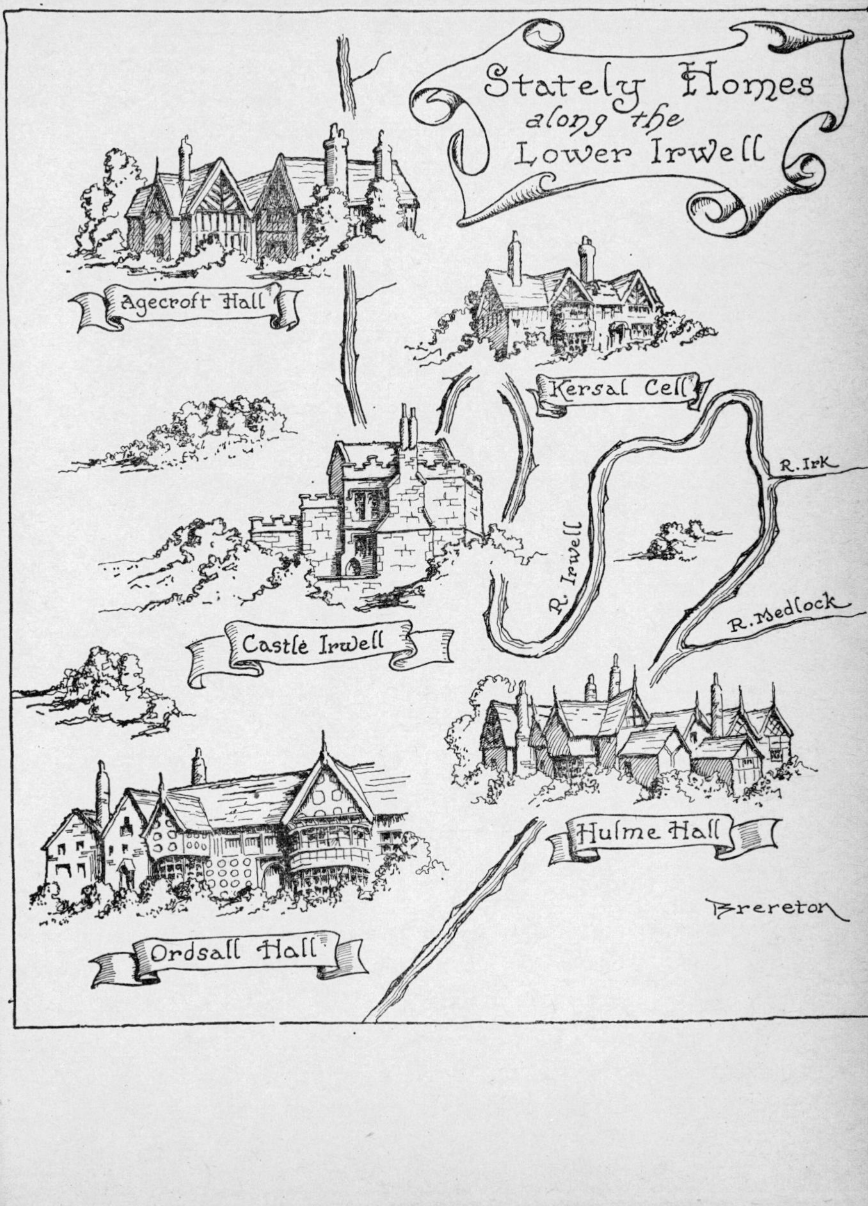

Stately Homes
along the
Lower Irwell
Agecroft Hall
Kersal Cell
R. Irk
Castle Irwell
R. Irwell
R. Medlock
Hulme Hall
Ordsall Hall
Brereton

Harrison Ainsworth, a nineteenth-century author whose book *Rookwood* started the legend of Dick Turpin's ride to York, wrote a romantic novel called *Guy Fawkes* which many believed to be based on fact, and in which a glamorous heroine, eighteen-year-old Vivian Radcliffe, received her lover, Catesby, in her father's absence. At Ordsall he met Guy Fawkes who had come secretly to ask for the Radcliffes' support in his famous plot. When soldiers raided the house Catesby and Vivian were saved by Humphrey Chetham, founder of the college and library that bears his name, who led them through a tunnel under the moat.

In 1875 the house became one of the first working-men's clubs, the great hall being transformed into a gymnasium; an upper room became a billiards room and part of the garden was laid out as a bowling green. Several rooms were also rented to a Methodist Sunday School. In 1959 Salford Corporation bought the hall from its latest owner, the Trustees of the Tatton Estate, and it was opened in May 1972 as a folk museum.

The house now faces a row of terraced dwellings dating from about the beginning of the present century. Farther up the street a tall block of new flats is visible and a short distance away is the great sprawl of Manchester's dockland. Behind the house a long rampart of old warehouses blocks from sight the Irwell, and it is difficult to believe that from the windows of this house the stony hills of Derbyshire could once be seen.

On the side of the red sandstone hill that rose from the river near Ordsall there was a natural cavern known as Great Ordsall Cave. Most historians accept that this had been used by the Romans as a place of worship dedicated to Mithrais. Later it was converted by the Saxons into a temple of the Norse god Woden. After the decline of Woden it was taken over by a colony of Christian monks, but it was still called Woden's Cave until late in the nineteenth century, when it was either filled in or disappeared through some natural subsidence.

The visitor today will search in vain for Agecroft Hall, mentioned though it is in many historical records as part of the Manor of Agecroft which Joan de Tetlow brought for her dowry to her marriage with Richard de Langley in the mid-fourteenth century.

This half-timbered mansion was built on the defensive plan in the form of a complete quadrangle about 35 yards square. The period was one in which the fortified medieval castle was no longer so necessary, but the houses of the rich could still fear attack from their neighbours and so needed a defensive construction. Agecroft contained about fifty rooms and was surrounded by a moat which later became a fish pond. Originally there were open galleries overlooking the courtyard on all four sides, but at some later date these were enclosed, as was the cloister beneath them. An item of special interest was the badge, just below the centre window of the upper storey at the front of the house, believed to be the emblem of Richard II with a white hart couchant.

The interior was altered considerably as time went on but some special features remained untouched, including a window which bore the red and white rose emblems of

Floods at the Crescent, Salford. A print from the "Illustrated Times", November 24, 1866.

Salford Local History Library

Contemporary prints of flood damage in Salford. Above, "The Rope Walk", Springfield Lane; below, Lower Broughton. **Salford Local History Library**

York and Lancaster. The flower stems in this were entwined between the letters HE and the date 1485, this being the year in which Henry VII married Elizabeth, daughter of Edward IV, thus uniting the rival houses.

Above the door to the drawing-room were eight figures carved in bold relief and representing War and Peace. These had earlier been removed from the pulpit in the private chapel of the house.

The existence of Agecroft Hall was threatened in the early nineteenth century when there was a proposal to demolish it to make way for a railway line from Manchester to Bolton. A Mr. Buck, a local exponent of conservation before his time, spent £5,000 of his own money on a campaign to save the hall for posterity and eventually succeeded in persuading the railway company to divert their line.

The hall fell into decay, but in 1925 there came a saviour in the shape of one Thomas C. Williams, jnr. of Richmond, U.S.A. A remote ancestor of Mr. Williams was a Welshman who had emigrated to the New World in 1607, seeking a new life in Virginia. Now his descendant had arrived on a return pilgrimage to the Old World, bringing with him a long-cherished dream of creating an English mansion in his home state—and by the Irwell he found the neglected hall of the long-departed Langleys.

Thomas Williams was facinated by the stories and legends surrounding the hall, such as the legend that the tale of the babes in the wood had been inspired by an actual incident during the reign of Edward III.

Pining of grief for the death of her lord in the French wars, Lady Joan de Langley had left her young son in wardship to her late husband's patron John of Gaunt, Duke of Lancaster. On the morning of the Feast of Ascension, in 1374, the villainous Robert de Holland "with many others assembled with him, armed in breast-plates and with swords, and bows and arrows, by force took possession of the said lordship of the duke, in defiance of the Sheriff, and to the contempt of the Lord Duke".

Exactly how the noble Duke was occupying himself while this dastardly business was taking place is not recorded, but it appears that young Langley and his sister escaped to the shelter of the forest which then covered the slopes of the Irwell Valley; there they were cared for by loyal retainers until Lancaster rescued them.

Thomas Williams, hearing these stories, determined to save the hall from becoming an ignoble ruin by the banks of a polluted Irwell. He bought it and had it carefully dismantled, including the minstrels' gallery and the mullioned bay window which measured 8 yards in length by 3 yards high. Every beam and stone was carefully numbered and crated and shipped across the Atlantic.

Now Agecroft Hall stands as a tourist attraction in Sulgrave Road, Richmond, Virginia, on a bluff overlooking the James River and surrounded by landscaped gardens and terraces. Both house and gardens are opened to the public and are looked after by the Agecroft Association.

Where the house had been for more than four centuries on the Irwell there now rise the cooling towers of Agecroft Power Station, in the entrance hall of which is a picture of the hall before its removal. There are also two excellent illustrations of the house in Margaret Chapman's book *Lancashire Halls* (Frank Graham, 1971).

Close to Agecroft Bridge there still exists another stately relic of the past—Kersal Cell, once the home of the Byroms. This house also dates from the fourteenth century when it was occupied by a colony of the Reformed Benedictine monks of Cluny, hence the name "Cell". It is now a country club, maintained in an elegant manner preserving its historical authenticity. There are worse fates than this for gracious houses.

Today, the long room on the ground floor where the monks once ate is used for dancing. The Prince Charles dining-room still has a row of lion heads along one wall with iron pipes in their mouths through which the monks used to make their confession to their abbot in the next room. Upstairs, John Byrom's bedroom is an extension to the bar. In winter it is warmed by a blazing log fire in the same iron fireplace that the poet knew. Through the bedroom window one can look across the green expanse of the Littleton Playing Fields towards the river.

A house few seemed to have loved was Castle Irwell which stood on a rise of ground within the great loop of the river encompassing the racecourse. Home of the Fitzgerald family, it was not really a castle but a large castellated brick house constructed in 1826 and described in the New Manchester Racecourse Souvenir Programme of that year as "unsightly, unsanitary and unsafe". It was pulled down in 1900 after the racecourse company had acquired ownership of the ground.

Another large and important dwelling, which no longer stands, was Hulme Hall. Built around a system of internal courtyards, it stood at the junction of Irwell and Medlock, near to where the Romans had their fort. Used as the setting for Harrison Ainsworth's first romantic novel, *Sir John Chiverton,* it was built on a sandstone rock that overhung the Irwell and was surrounded by a line of beech trees that gave way to green meadows. Steep paths wound down to the river and a sloping ledge called Fisherman's Rock. The central towers of the hall with their conical roofs formed a landmark visible for miles.

Hulme Hall was demolished in 1848 to make way for buildings in connection with the Bridgewater Canal. Some of the carved oak panelling was saved and taken to Worsely Hall where it graces one of the rooms.

6

SHIPPING AND NAVIGATION

The dream of a navigable waterway from the heart of the Manchester/Salford region down to the sea at Liverpool was an ancient one. It haunted for generations the imaginations of the merchants who dwelt along the Irwell's banks.

The Irwell and the Mersey were wide enough for the barges of the eighteenth century; that greater vision of huge ocean-going steamers plying along a canal was for the distant future. Even the barges could not traverse the length of the Irwell to its junction with the Mersey because of the numerous weirs, sandbanks and narrow bends. The river's course on the map is a tortuous one; it frequently snakes back upon itself as if reluctant to advance and lose at last its identity to the superior Mersey.

In 1720 a group of merchants having at last grown impatient with the length and the dangers of that tedious journey along the muddy tracks that counted for roads, formed themselves into a company and persuaded Parliament to pass an Act authorizing them to "Make and keep the rivers Mersey and Irwell navigable from Manchester to Liverpool for boats, barges, lighters and other vessels".

The Act stated that this would be "beneficial for trade, advantageous to the poor, and convenient for the carrying of coal, cannel, stone, timber and other goods, wares and merchandise; and would tend very much to the employing and maintenance of watermen and seamen and be a means of preserving the highway".

The Company, referred to in the Act as the Undertakers, were further authorized to "scour, enlarge and straighten the rivers Mersey and Irwell, to make new cuts for shortening distances, to cut down trees, to build bridges and form sluices, to take materials from adjoining fields, to alter bridges, turn highways, pull down mills or weirs, to make towing paths".

Armed with such powers the "Undertakers" must indeed have felt like gods, empowered to remould the landscape on a scale never attempted before. There were, however, just a few restrictions. For example, the Act stated that

> The waters of the rivers shall not be raised or dammed up to such a height as to hinder the working of corn mills; that no wharf shall be built within a mile of Bank Quay, Warrington, without consent.

The Act also specified that "coal, cannel, stone, timber

and other goods shall pay duties to the Undertakers not exceeding $\frac{3}{4}$*d.* per ton".

After their great task was completed, the Undertakers evolved into the Mersey and Irwell Navigation Company, and by the 1750s this Company was running a regular service from Manchester to Liverpool.

The vessels were sometimes pulled by horses but more often by men. It took three or four men to do the job which was probably less arduous than it sounds. They were not slaves, lashed to labour as in some Roman galley, but reasonably free men working for a wage, and they were not pulling on the towropes all the time. If a suitable wind should arise then the big square sails which gave these vessels a curiously Eastern appearance, would be set and the men would jump aboard to ride freely.

Unlike the later Ship Canal the Irwell was so variable in its windings that no matter from what quarter the wind blew there were certain to be periods when the sail would be unusable; in the Crescent at Salford, for instance, or the great loop round what is now the old racecourse in Broughton.

By 1766 there were fourteen boats trading from Manchester and six from Salford; but surprisingly, the business proved to be something less than the El Dorado that the original Undertakers had visualized. For its first fifty years the Mersey and Irwell Navigation failed to make a profit.

In 1776 the owners, in desperation, offered the Company to the Duke of Bridgewater for £5,000 but the

Duke vigorously competing with the Company for trade, refused, and thereafter the Mersey and Irwell Navigation continued in business under the name of Old Quay Company.

There were two types of craft on the run to Warrington and Runcorn: the Packet Boats and the Swift Packet Boats. The former were lightly built, roomy, measuring about sixty feet in length by fourteen feet in the beam and were drawn by two or more horses. The cabins and wide decks accommodated many passengers with their luggage and still left room for some cargo. These boats were not in a hurry and would oblige passengers by stopping at any of the numerous little local landing stages.

The Swift Packet Boats were smaller, more slender of line and for passengers only. They were drawn by two or three good horses ridden by red-jacketed jockeys, the leader carrying a horn to warn anyone on the towpath to give way. They travelled at a fast trot, even a gallop on occasions, and the general speed of the boat was equal to that of the mail coaches. On May Day the horses would be decorated with ribbons and bells, their brasses, and harness polished with loving care, reflecting the sun.

There were no regular starting times for these river expresses; they would begin their journey at any time of day or night in order to catch the first ebb of the tide at Runcorn, where passengers for Liverpool would transfer to larger boats going with the tide down the Mersey to the sea. When a strong wind blew, the big square sails would be hoisted. The bows would ripple through the water and on shore the horses would have to gallop to keep up.

In 1810, after many years of strenuous opposition to the idea, the Old Quay Company formed an alliance with their younger rival, the Bridgewater Trustees, in order to put an end to the ruinous competition that had developed between them. From then on the two companies charged identical rates.

When the railways came and brought dangerous land-based competition, every effort had to be made to improve the navigation and in 1840 a costly project was carried out. This involved deepening and widening the river so that it became navigable for vessels of 300 tons. A system was instituted of placing goods in bond in warehouses belonging to the Company.

Under the then novel heading of "The Port of Manchester" the *Manchester Guardian,* in 1841, announced that a ship had arrived direct from Dublin with a cargo of potatoes, and was discharging at the Old Quay Company's Wharf.

The Editor wrote

> The vessel, the *Mary,* under Captain John Hill, having discharged her cargo, will clear and sail this day direct for Dublin with a cargo of coals from the colliery of Mr. Fitzgerald at Pendleton. Such are probably the small beginnings of Manchester's future greatness as one of the ports of the United Kingdom.

Shortly afterwards the following prophetic little song was published:

The Union Flag is flying
By the Company's wharf Old Quay,
And the *Mary* of Dublin lying
Unloading her Murphies today.

In the Irish Sea I hailed her
As I stood in the Packet Boat,
With equal pride I never saw
A merchant sloop afloat.

Your name? The *Mary,* Captain Hill!
Your cargo potatoes, sir,
Where from Dublin, wither bound?
The port of Manchester!

Eighteen hundred and forty,
October the twentieth day,
At half past four in the evening
She anchored at the Quay.

It always does my heart good
To see the Union Jack,
So here's success to *Mary*
And soon may she come back.

And soon may scores of others
Perform the trip with her,
And trade and commerce double
In noble Manchester.

* * *

Although Friday, February 29, 1828, was not a holiday for the workers of Manchester and Salford, hundreds of middleclass citizens who could afford to take time off, and a percentage of the unemployed eager for a diversion, made their way to the river at the boat-building yard just above Regent Bridge in the early afternoon of a day cold but dry and sunny. They went to watch the launching of the *Emma,* the biggest cargo vessel ever to be made on the Irwell.

The proud ship lay on its stocks, with about 300 specially invited guests on deck, the ladies in their finery with billowing skirts and colourful bonnets.

It was a brave scene—so suddenly to erupt into tragedy. Flags and streamers fluttered gaily along the quayside and on boats drifting along the river, waiting for this giant to slide into its watery kingdom.

Distant cannon crashed forth with a thunderous salute—the only effective means of momentarily obliterating the band of the 9th Regiment determinedly blasting out with a mixture of jolly tunes and military marches.

Several dignitaries made lengthy and tedious speeches, and then the two daughters of Mr Brereton-Grime, agent of the New Quay Company, giggly and self-concious of the fame thrust upon them, stepped forward and each sent a bottle of champagne to break against the ill-fated vessel's bows.

A roar of cheers from the crowd, a roll of drums from the band and the *Emma* slid from her stocks, dipped gently into the water—and plunged straight across the river to strike the Salford bank. In a second she had turned on her side, throwing her passengers from the crowded, suddenly sloping decks, into the black water.

Men on the bank dived in and began the work of rescue. A number of the victims were drowned through clinging hysterically to each other in groups. Women's bonnets and men's top hats floated in scores like funeral wreaths among the struggling bodies. Twenty-two dead were pulled out on the Salford side and sixteen on the Manchester side.

One of the rescuers was drowned, while another, an heroic fishmonger who had stripped off most of his clothes and dived in time and again, suffered a sad fate. On returning to the bank for the last time he found that his clothes had been stolen! Exposure and subsequent exhaustion brought on a serious illness from which he died a few weeks later.

It was said afterwards that some died, not so much through water in the lungs as from poisoning by the gasworks refuse which had not at that time been cleaned up.

Such was the fate of the *Emma,* and of those who, for a few moments, had hoped to sail in her.

Most of the craft that plied along the Irwell were built on its banks, even, in 1852, a new type of lifeboat. This was of a tubular construction, created in an iron-works opposite Manchester Cathedral. It was the invention of two Welshmen, a father and son named Richardson who came all the way from Bala for the facilities offered by the ironworks. They spent a fortune in their efforts to win a competition for a new design of lifeboat to replace the so-called "self-righting" lifeboat which in practice often proved unstable and failed to live up to its name.

On the Irwell the Richardsons launched an original type of craft consisting of two watertight iron tubes each measuring nearly forty feet in length by thirty inches in diameter and set about three feet apart. The crew were intended to ride on a platform consisting of a rope net-work fixed over the tubes.

The Richardsons failed to win the competition, probably because the judges were instinctively looking for a boat whereas what the Welshmen had made was more like a raft. Nevertheless, the unique stability of their design attracted a body of supporters who caused it to be transported from the river to Rhyl, on the coast of North Wales, where it was thoroughly tested and finally adopted by the lifeboat station there in 1856. Seven years later a second version was made and established at New Brighton where it remained in use for thirty-five years and took part in many rescues, including the rescue of a third tubular boat which had been adopted by the Liverpool Harbour Board!

The lifeboats made by the two Welshmen on the Irwell did at least have some measure of success, although they were never very popular with the lifeboatmen who had to man them and who spent most of their time soaking wet!

7

BRINDLEY AND THE CANAL DUKE

In 1770 a traveller named Arthur Young published a work entitled *Six Months Tour Through the North of England* in which he described the horrors of a journey from Wigan to Preston:

> I know not in the whole of England terms sufficiently expressive to describe this infernal road. Let me seriously caution all travellers who may accidentally propose to travel this terrible country to avoid it as they would the devil, for a thousand to one but that they break their necks or their limbs by overthrowing or breaking down. They will meet with ruts which I have actually measured, four feet deep, and floating with mud only from a wet summer. What, therefore, must it be after a winter?

It was such conditions as these that rendered difficult the task of transporting to Manchester and Salford the coal that had been mined in the Irwell valley from the earliest times. Although the coal seams were relatively easy to reach in this area it had to be carried on the backs of pack-horses to the nearest point on the Irwell and then loaded on to barges for the journey downstream. Two hundredweight of coal on a horse cost 10*d.* at the pit near Worsley, but by the time the load reached a landing stage in Manchester it often cost at least as much as that in transport charges. In severe winters, when the coal was needed most, the traffic was often halted altogether by snow-bound tracks or icy conditions on the river.

All these problems were eventually solved, and the day came when coal from Worsley was sold in Manchester at 4*d.* for a bag of 120 lb.! The apparent miracle was wrought by the partnership of two highly eccentric characters: the Duke of Bridgewater and an uncouth, illiterate peasant's son from the Peak District of Derbyshire, one James Brindley, who, by some freakish biological mutation, also happened to be an engineer of genius.

This fascinating "rough diamond" was born in a poor cottage in the windy, barren hills of the Peak. He had no formal education and his mechanical ability came, as he phrased it, "natural like". Unlettered, blunt of speech and manner, Brindley found it easier to carry out a technical design than to communicate his ideas to others. When a task presented difficulties he would often retire to bed for several days. There his retentive memory and ready understanding of mechanical theory would enable him to formulate the most complex plans without

Barton aqueduct from the North-east. In the foreground is the old Navigation Lock.

Barton aqueduct from Barton Bridge.

F

Brindley's draining scheme at Wet-Earth Colliery

the help of drawings which he was unable to execute. His estimates of expenses, however, were said to have been often very hazy.

At the age of twenty-six he started in business as a wheelwright, and in 1752 attracted the attention of engineers by designing a water-engine for the draining of coal mines. His design for a new type of silk mill brought him in 1759 to the notice of the Duke of Bridgewater.

In his youth the Canal Duke (1736–1803), as he was later called, had led the normal wild and hedonistic life of his class. He took the Grand Tour of Europe, wining, wenching, gambling; but his relations with women tended to be unfortunate and after returning to England and being involved in several broken romances he fled from his London residence to the rural shelter of Worsley Hall, where he proceeded to spend a solitary existence trying to think out schemes whereby the coal from his mines could be conveyed at a better profit to the populated regions in the lower reaches of the Irwell.

That first meeting between the brooding recluse of Worsley Hall and the rough commoner from the hills began a strange association which was to result in the creation of one of the great engineering feats of the eighteenth century, though the genius whose work it was received little in the way of monetary reward.

The Duke was accustomed to being treated with deference and courtesy by people of Brindley's class. It took him some time to get used to being called simply "Duke", and a bit longer still to the unfamiliar experience of being told not to "talk such damned nonsense". But this oddly-assorted pair managed to get along with each other.

The Duke had visualized a canal from Worsley to the Irwell, which would still have left transport subject to the vagaries of the river being in many places too low during drought periods, besides the usual obstacles of winter ice.

Brindley explained that he would dig a canal all the way to Manchester and take it *across* the Irwell at Barton, the river's nearest point to Worsley. It would be ten miles long and he proposed to avoid the necessity for locks—which he considered to be bad engineering—by cutting the canal all the way on the level with an aqueduct over the Irwell which would be made watertight by Brindley's favourite method of clay puddling. He was so fond of this that, years later, as he lay dying, his last words were said to have been "puddle it, puddle it".

Puddling consisted of putting together several layers of well-tempered clay mixed with sand and water, the total thickness being about three feet. In his book *The Bridgewater Millions* Bernard Falk mentions that a variation of puddling was recommended for making Anderson air-raid shelters watertight during World War II.

The Duke consulted one of the most eminent engineers of the day who laughed when told of Brindley's proposed aqueduct and said "I have often heard of castles in the air, but never before saw where any of them was to be erected".

Nevertheless, something in Brindley's character seemed to fascinate the Duke, and he fell in with the plan.

Brindley then spent some weeks on what he called in his colloquial way "ochilor recconitoring".

In due course there was presented to Parliament an "Act to enable the Most Noble Francis, Duke of Bridgewater, to make a navigable cut or canal from a certain place in the township of Salford to or near Worsley Mill in the Manor of Worsley."

A Parliamentary Committee expressed at first considerable doubts about the feasibility of taking a canal over a river, but the doubts were dispelled when Brindley went to London and gave in the Commons one of his "ochilor demonstrations". He took along a hunk of cheese from which he cut a model of his aqueduct, and with a mess of clay and water showed them how puddling would make it watertight.

The Act was passed, and the Duke managed to raise sufficient money to start work, though a great deal more was eventually needed. As usual, Brindley's estimate was somewhat unrealistic.

Brindley moved into Worsley Hall to live and the Duke limited his own expenses to a mere £400 per year, selling all except two of his horses and dismissing the servants except one manservant who had to cover the whole range of domestic chores.

For two years Brindley and the Duke lived together in the Hall, most of its rooms shuttered and dusty; they argued, schemed and frequently quarrelled as the work progressed. Experts scoffed, and the locals said "This 'ere Brindley's a-ruinin' o' th' Duke".

Because of the expense of the undertaking Brindley

accepted a fee of only one guinea per week. Sometimes he had to go to London on business connected with the purchase of supplies, which took four to five days each way on horseback and for this he charged the Duke £4 8*s*.

There were occasions when money looked like running out altogether. When this happened, the Duke would mount one of his two remaining horses and deliver letters asking for loans from his neighbours. Sometimes the two of them would sit brooding over shilling dinners at a local hostelry, wondering where next week's money was to come from to pay the army of navvies; but somehow the money continued to be found and the work went on.

At last on July 17, 1761, the water was poured into the canal for the first time, but Brindley was not there to see it. In an agony of nervous prostration, afraid that his great idea would fail, he had retired to bed.

The *Manchester Mercury* afterwards reported the pouring ceremony:

> On Friday last his Grace the Duke of Bridgewater with the Earl of Staffordshire and several other gentlemen, came to Barton to see the water turned into the canal over the River Irwell, which drew together a large number of spectators and it is with pleasure that we can inform the public that the operation answered the now sanguine expectations of everyone present.
>
> As soon as the water had risen to the level of the canal a large boat carrying upwards of 50 tons was towed along the new part of the canal over arches

across the River Irwell which was so finely secured and compact that not a single drop of water could be perceived to ooze through, although the surface of the canal is 38 feet above the river.

The good news was carried to Brindley who rose in relief from his bed.

Later that year a reader wrote in a letter to the *Manchester Mercury:*

At Barton Bridge the ingenious Mr. Brindley has created a navigable canal in the air; for it is as high as the tops of the trees. While I was seeing it with a mixture of wonder and delight, four barges passed me in the space of about three minutes, two of them being chained together and dragged by two horses who went on the terraces of the canal, whereas, I must own, I durst hardly venture, as I almost trembled to behold the Irwell beneath me.

The first boatload of coal, on the day of the canal's opening, had been unloaded on the Duke's wharves at Knott Mill, in the centre of Manchester, where a huge fair was held to celebrate the event. The fair was afterwards held annually and became known as the Knott Mill Fair.

Visitors came from all over the world to see the wonder of Brindley's aqueduct, and the engineer's fame was established.

Brindley went on to do more work for the Duke. He

constructed miles of underground waterway for the draining of the coalpits. Along these subterranean rivers the coal was floated on long narrow boats to the basin at Worsley. While tunnelling a hill at Worsley to give access to the pits he also invented a new type of mortar for use with his masonry.

The canal at Worsley today, used largely by pleasure craft, is discoloured, not by industrial pollution as many people imagine, but from seepage of water from the underground channels that Brindley dug.

Anyone looking at a modern map may search in vain for the place where Brindley's aqueduct crosses the Irwell, for the aqueduct is shown as crossing the Manchester Ship Canal where a long section of the Irwell has been incorporated into the Canal and where the name of the river has disappeared from the maps.

In fact, it is not even Brindley's aqueduct which crosses the Canal at Barton today. The original structure survived for 130 years and, when the Ship Canal was built, it was replaced by that even greater engineering miracle a steel swing bridge which turns, carrying the water with it, allowing vessels from all parts of the world to pass by.

Brindley spent a further four years working on an extension of the canal to Runcorn, on the Mersey Estuary. Despite his belief that locks constituted bad engineering, he had no alternative but to construct them, for he was dealing with a different terrain. The Runcorn extension opened for traffic on January 10, 1773, and was widely used for a century thereafter, both for cargo traffic and passenger—and sometimes pleasure also.

Brindley did not see the opening ceremony of this canal, either, for he died in the previous year at the age of fifty-six.

Samuel Smiles (1812–1904), biographer of engineers, wrote:

> We doubt whether mere hard work ever killed any man, or whether Brindley's labours, extraordinary though they were, would have shortened his life, but for the more trying conditions of the engineer's vocation—irregular living, exposure to all weathers, long fasting and then, perhaps, heavy feeding when the nervous system was exhausted, together with habitual disregard of ordinary physical needs. Soaked while out on a job, and put into damp sheets at an inn, diabetes developed and he died shortly. He had created 365 miles of canals.

At Throstle Nest Lock, on the fringes of what is now the Trafford Park Industrial Estate, Brindley's canal swings in a wide curve and comes quite close to the Irwell. It was a regular habit of pleasure parties from Manchester or Salford to row along the river to this point and then to carry their boats up the bank to the canal along which they would continue to Sale or Altrincham or, in the other direction, to Worsley itself; all the time travelling through country places where the grass was still green, the trees tall and proud and the air fit to breathe.

On the journey to Altrincham the rowers would pass

lush green meadows, strawberry gardens, and tea gardens where they could pull in for a rest and refresh themselves with that ancient English custom of the "afternoon tea".

During a visit to Manchester and Salford Queen Victoria and Prince Albert took a trip on the canal in a State Barge constructed specially for the occasion.

In the nineteenth century there developed a regular service between Knott Mill and Runcorn by a fleet of so-called Fly-boats. These vessels had fine bows with high scroll-shaped iron blades to sever any hindering tow-ropes. They were roomy and comfortable with big-windowed cabins for protection against inclement weather.

The last time a passenger service operated on the Bridgewater was for a few brief days during a bus strike in 1962 when an enterprising barge owner fitted out one of his boats and advertised the morning journey from Altrincham into Manchester and back in the evening. Passengers enjoyed a unique morning sail from the Cheshire suburbia into the region of crumbling offices and warehouses that today line the banks of canal and river.

8

COTTON AND THE PEOPLE OF THE MILLS

In the seventeenth century the manufacture of cloth in the Manchester area became well established because local authorities allowed clothiers to cut timber for looms from the woods at only 4*d*. per annum. By the 1650s the production of sackcloth, tapes and woollen friezes was the cause of much prosperity. Undoubtedly the Flemish weavers, who had come to the region in the fourteenth century, brought their talents and influence to bear in this business.

Then cotton began to arrive. In 1727 Daniel Defoe visited Manchester and commented "The grand manufacture which has so much raised this town is that of cotton and all its varieties".

King Cotton had chosen his kingdom and the long reign was begun.

There were sound reasons why south Lancashire provided a favourable environment for the weaving and making up of cotton goods. Throughout most of the

Elizabethan and the Stuart periods the incorporated towns of Britain had had regulations imposed upon them through the guilds which tended to be of a protectionist nature and helped to inhibit industrial development, especially in the field of textiles. For example, there was a limit on the number of looms which any one family was allowed to operate, and there were property qualifications which limited the number of apprentices. Such restrictions did not apply to Manchester on the Irwell or to Bolton on the Roch, neither of which was an incorporated town. Private enterprise was thus enabled to flourish in this region to a greater extent than elsewhere, and there seems little doubt that this was a major factor in the development of the cotton and textile industry once the raw material began to be imported from the East.

The wool trade flourished for some time yet, and in 1750 the fatness of eels caught in the river Irk was attributed to the "grease and oils from woollen cloth milled in it", though the scientific probability of this theory seems open to doubt.

By the 1780s the woollen weavers were leaving the county, most of them apparently going to Wiltshire. Nevertheless, cotton was still a cottage industry. The spinning and weaving was done either in the home or in small workshops employing about half a dozen people. Merchants carried their goods about the countryside on horseback, visiting particularly the numerous country fairs and the village shops.

Change came quickly. Mills employing some scores of

workers began to be established along the banks of the Irwell and the faster-flowing sections of its many brooks so that the power of running water could be used to turn water-wheels. The invention of Edmund Cartwright's power loom in 1784 had a great impact and Watt's steam engine soon followed. The greatest of all mankind's revolutions had begun—along the Irwell.

One of the worst of the social changes was the widening gulf between master and man. Their reasonably amicable relationship was soon to be destroyed. Coincidentally with the invention of steam-power a new wave of enclosures of the common lands into private property took place between 1760 and 1820, and this drove the peasants off the land into the towns, where the "dark satanic mills" now rising along the Irwell and its tributaries were waiting to suck them into the great turmoil of the weaving sheds.

Children were early fodder for the machines; but an Act of 1819 forbade the employment of children on night shifts, and later Acts reduced hours of work for those aged nine to thirteen to only forty-eight hours weekly, while the thirteen to eighteen-year-olds could work for sixty-nine hours. There was also an Act which stated that children must have two hours of compulsory education per day.

For a long time the various Acts of Parliament had very little effect in practice as no attempt was made to enforce them. Few workers were prepared to risk taking their employers to court for breaking the law. An investigation of one mill revealed that the children *were* receiving their compulsory "education"—in the coal hole from a fireman who himself could not read!

In 1833 factory inspectors were appointed for the first time; and although for some years they were few in number they did gradually force the employers to an ever greater extent to obey the law. In 1819 there was published a Government Report in which the following passage occurred:

> Prolonged and exhausting labour, continued from day to day, and from year to year, is not calculated to develop the intellectual or moral faculties of man. The dull routine of a ceaseless drudgery, in which the same mechanical process is incessantly repeated, resembles the torment of Sisyphus. The toil, like the rock, recoils perpetually on the wearied operative.

Not everyone, however, saw life in the mills in gloomy terms. A certain Mr. W. Cooke-Taylor, writing his *Notes of a Tour in the Manufacturing Districts of Lancashire* in 1842, preferred to wear rose-coloured glasses.

> How a painter would have envied the sight which broke upon my waking eyes this morning! To my right is one of the tributaries of the Irwell, winding through the depths of a richly wooded and precipitous valley, or rather ravine; the sun's rays, glinting from the waters, come like flashes through every opening in the foliage. . . . The Turton Mill is built in the bottom of the ravine, just under the owner's residence, from

which, however, it is separated by the little stream I have already noticed. . . . The interior of Mr. Ashworth's mill does not differ materially from that of many other well-regulated mills which I have visited. I mention this because of the burst of sentimental sympathy for the condition of factory operatives which, a few years ago, frightened the isle out of its propriety. The conditions of health in the mills that I have generally examined are exceedingly favourable. The working rooms are lofty, spacious and well ventilated, kept at an equable temperature and scrupulously clean. There is nothing in sight, sound or smell to offend the most fastidious taste . . . crowding is physically impossible. I should be well content to have as large a proportion of room and air in my own study as a cotton spinner in any of the mills of Lancashire . . . I must remark that the toil is not very great . . . the heaviest part of the labour is executed by the steam-engine or water-wheel and there are many intervals of rest . . . a cotton operative is at rest one minute out of every three during the period of his nominal employment.

One who observed the Lancashire scene and wrote about it from a different point of view was Frederick Engels, whose father owned a mill in Pendleton. Frederick was an angry young man of his time, as indeed anyone with a conscience and sensitivity could not fail to be in the 1840s. Unfortunately, anger tends to distort the vision, and the young German lacked the scientific approach of his friend Karl Marx to whom he frequently sent cheques to help the ageing philosopher continue his researches in the British Museum.

Some of the facts provided by Engels undoubtedly went into the making of *Das Kapital,* yet the young revolutionary, as he strolled about Manchester and Salford, observing the dismal factories that cluttered the Irwell's banks, was not above bending those facts sometimes.

W. O. Henderson and W. H. Chaloner, who translated Engels, have pointed out that sometimes he would quote a report or account of life in the mills and factories which was gruesome and accurate enough, while omitting to mention that it might be thirty years or more out of date and that the conditions described did not necessarily apply any longer.

Engels was typical of the very emotional left-wingers whose visions get in the way of their reasoning. Their eyes fill with tears as they see a glorious picture of the workers rising at last to seize their heritage.

In 1844, returning to Germany after his first spell of exile in Manchester, working at his father's mill, Engels prophesied with certainty the imminent coming of a workers' revolt along the Irwell that would be far greater than the French Revolution. On a later visit in the 1870s he was still expecting it. And in 1917 Lenin, too, was expecting it. . . .

If Frederick Engels was guilty of manipulating time, then a certain Mr. Holland Hoole stands accused of the even greater sins of hypocrisy and blind aversion to facts. In 1832 this gentleman wrote a letter to the Chancellor

Stage Buildings from the Salford side of the river. The tower in the background is St. Mary's Church. From a water colour, 1877.

The Crescent, Salford, 1967. **Salford Local History Libr**

of the Exchequer protesting about a proposal then before Parliament, for reducing the hours of work from sixty-nine to fifty-eight per week. It is hardly necessary to add that Mr. Hoole was himself a mill-owner.

He began with a hymn of praise for the virtues of life in t'mill by explaining that:

> In some of the villages near Manchester where there are no factories, the inhabitants are notoriously more immoral and degraded than in places where the people are chiefly occupied in factory labour. Nor are we too far from the meads of Cheshire to know that agricultural labourers are not less vicious, to say the least, than our much misrepresented factory people. I am at a loss to learn how any improvement in morals is to be the necessary consequence of a reduction in the hours of labour.
>
> Much has been said respecting the heat of the rooms and the noxious effluvium to which operatives are supposed to be subjected. It is true that in what are usually called "fine spinning" mills a somewhat high degree of heat is considered beneficial to the work, and in such mills 80 degrees of Fahrenheit is not unusual, and may even be sometimes exceeded, at the express request of the spinners themselves.[!]

The mental vision of the workers actually requesting temperatures in excess of 80°F is something of a strain on one's credulity. He continues:

> The number of such mills does not constitute more than one tenth of the actual number of factories, and in the other nine tenths no more heat is required than is needed for the comfort of the hands. In these latter, the variations of the temperature is very similar to that of an ordinary dwelling house, falling to 50°F in winter and rising to 70°F in summer.

It was fortunate for Mr. Hoole that he did not have to contend with shop stewards. His "average dwelling house temperature" would be the cause of a union walk-out today.

We can, however, take comfort in the knowledge that the morality of the workers in Mr. Hoole's own mills was well looked after, for, out of the 768 operatives employed there were 298 who attended Sunday School "without any influence or inducement on the part of their employer"!

That many of the mills were very hot indeed is evidenced by the fact that the hands often took off items of clothing immediately on arriving. In the course of a Parliamentary investigation in 1833 a female witness was asked:

> "When you come of a morning, do you take off some of your clothes?"
>
> "Yes, sir."
>
> "Do the piecers see one another take off their clothes?"
>
> "Yes, as fast as they come in they slip off nearly

all their clothes, and the girls put on their bishops (smocks)."

"What do you take off?"

"My hat, shawl, shoes and stockings."

"What do the lads take off?"

"Shoes, stockings, hat, coat, waistcoat; all works barefoot."

"Do the big lads see the big girls take off their stockings?"

"Yes, sir."

"Do the boys ever say anything naughty and pert?"

"Yes, some big boys is always doing it."

"Do the girls care about it?"

"Some doesn't like it; some doesn't mind it."

During the same investigation a youth was asked:

"Did the masters lick you?"

"I never worked with a master yet but what he licked me when I was late in the mornings. One master used to lick me of all colours if I was two minutes late. I've gone off from home half dressed, he used to be that savage. The spinners all beat the piecers. You see, it throws 'em behind of their work if the piecers a'nt there."

Another witness was asked what means were used to keep children awake. The investigators were told: "Sometimes they would tap them on the head, or nip them over the nose, or give them a pinch of snuff, or throw water in their faces."

* * *

There were three distinct stages in the growth of cotton and its effect upon the people who lived in the two great towns situated one on either side of the Irwell's lower reaches, and in the numerous smaller towns and villages in the upper reaches and also along the various tributary brooks and minor rivers.

First, there was the cottage industry stage in which a specific class of weavers arose; descended from yeomen farmers, these people would live in a small cottage and sell to the merchants the products of their hand looms. They would also have their small patch of ground on which they could grow at least some vegetables for their own use and perhaps have room for a few fruit trees. Some writers have described this period as idyllic. It was probably somewhat less than that, but at least it was reasonably healthy and infinitely preferable to the life that was to follow.

Stage two, in the first decades of the nineteenth century, saw the drift of the home weaver from the country cottage to the town hovel. The high cost of living caused by the wars with Napoleon, the growth of population which meant less work on the land for the sons of the home weavers because there were more hands than there were jobs; also the improvement in communications due to the growth of railways, made it more convenient for the merchants to concentrate their activities and businesses in the towns.

The decline of rural life had begun. Mankind, having

had no other sources of power for thousands of year than that of muscle, aided to a small extent by the harnessing of the wind and of rushing water, had discovered steam. Now the cities were to grow and grow, and suck the life and vitality out of the countryside.

The move to the towns along the Irwell disrupted the small communities in which the people were accustomed to live. The whole structure of rural society was shattered when they found themselves in dingy tenements grouped round dark courts, or in the rows of back-to-back terrace hovels that fanned out like a vast network of diseased veins from behind the mills that clung to the banks of the river.

Back in their country arcady the most important person in their lives had been the "squire". Obviously there were bad squires, but generally the relationship between the man in the mansion and the villagers in their cottages seems to have been at least one of a practical amiability. The squire knew his people personally. He was no remote aristocrat, rolling the cringing peasants in the dust beneath the wheels of his carriage. He attended their sports, their Morris dancing on May Day, their harvest thanksgiving and Easter rites. He was the dispenser of justice and of advice.

Now, all this was gone, along with the tribal security of the close-knit village community. In the city the transplanted villagers found themselves part of much larger groupings, and among strangers, too. The squire was replaced by the "master", the mill-owner. The old paternalism of the country way of life and the squirearchy may not have been an ideal relationship; certainly it did not appeal to anyone who liked to philosophize about social equality, but it was infinitely better than the new existence.

The master had no tradition of responsibility towards his people. To him they were so many hands to be exploited. He himself was usually a townsman, of the working class but with wits sharpened by the town environment, enlivened by ideas and driven by ambition. In short, the new capitalist class, conjured into being like a genie in a cloud of steam from James Watt's engine. Often with little education, despising his own class, envious of the gentry whose ranks he aspired to join, the new capitalist was determined to rise from amongst the common herd.

An observer of the times, James Phillips Kay, M.D., commented in a pamphlet entitled *The Moral and Physical Condition of the Working Classes Employed in Cotton Manufacture in Manchester* that:

> The villager had a physical constitution unimpaired by protracted toil in a heated and impure atmosphere, the fumes of the gin-shop, the low debauchery of the beer-house. He lived to a good ripe age, worked when necessity demanded; and if disposed to spend time and money in drinking could do so in a house as well conducted and as ordered as his own . . . a calm and equable flow of occupation alternating between the loom and the greensward . . . now a system of toil unbroken by rest or relaxation, for 14 or 16 hours, in

> a heated and crowded mill . . . an utter destruction of all social and domestic relations . . .

The old system of morality, which could be strictly observed in the small village setting where everybody knew what everbody else was doing, was an early casualty of the change, and the institution of marriage itself also apparently suffered some blows. Evidence given to the Factories Commission of 1833 stated that:

> Factory wives are incapable of laying out the money their husbands have earned to the best advantage. They are equally incapable of preparing victuals, in an economic and comfortable manner; and not infrequently as much money is spent on a Saturday's dinner as in other and better hands would have procured a dinner for two or three days. A working man is fortunate indeed who happens to marry a young woman who has been brought up in service. Her habits of cleanliness and knowledge of household duties secures him a comfortable home and economical management.

A poem of the period lamented the transition from the agricultural life to factory slavery:

> Come all you cotton weavers, your looms you may
> pull down,
> You must get employed in factories, in country or in
> town,

For our cotton masters have found out a shameful new
idea,
Their goods now wove by hand they're going to weave
by steam.
So come all you cotton weavers, you must leave your
looms,
For you must work in factories from morning until
noon.
You mustn't work in your gardens for two or three
hours a day,
For you must work at their command, and keep your
shuttles in play.

The nineteenth century abounded in charitable works. The poor were "always with us", practically an Act of God, and the leisured wives of the middle classes and of the aristocracy also, were able to fill in their time with various charities from caring for "fallen women" to the rescue of orphans. It was a good way of ensuring oneself of some reward in the hereafter. The main contribution of the churches in those times was to earn for Christianity a thoroughly bad name and for religion the Marxist description of "opiate of the people".

In 1844, Leon Faucher, a visitor from France, gave his own view of Manchester:

> All the houses, all the streets, resemble each other; and yet this uniformity is in the midst of confusion. On closer examination, however, a certain approximation

to order is apparent. Manchester is situated at the confluence of a little river, the Irwell, swollen by the waters of the Irk, and of a brook called the Medlock. The Irwell separates Manchester from its principal suburb—the old town which has given its name to the hundred of Salford. On the left bank of the river is another suburb, Chorlton-upon-Medlock, which in 1801, numbered only 675 inhabitants, and which now contains 30,000. The manufactories and machine shops form as it were, a girdle around the town, and follow the courses of the streams. Factories, seven storeys in height, rear their lofty fronts along the banks of the Irwell, and along the borders of the canals, which, penetrating into the town, form an interior navigation.

Even in those grim times, however, there were individuals of compassion and sensitivity who were horrified at the sufferings of the many and who fought to improve conditions. One of these was Michael Sadler, M.P. (1780–1835), who in 1832 introduced the Ten Hour Bill designed to reduce the hours of work for children to fifty-eight. Parliament insisted on setting up a Select Committee, but this came to an end and the Bill itself lapsed when Parliament was dissolved at the end of the year. Shortly afterwards Sadler was defeated in a by-election, but in 1833 Lord Ashley, another reformer, reintroduced the Bill. There were further delaying tactics and Parliament set up a Royal Factories Commission to make a thorough investigation.

On a visit to the Irwell region the Commission had the following petition presented to it:

To the Commissioners appointed by the King to inquire into the state of Factory Labour.

Gentlemen,—We, children employed in the factories of Manchester, beg leave to present to you this our humble and respectful memorial. We implore your pity and compassion for our sufferings for the great weight of labour thrown on our young limbs,—for the long duration of that labour daily, mostly in the close air of a heated room,—for the weakness it brings upon us while we are little, and the sickness and deformity which fall upon many of us,—for the overwhelming fatigue which benumbs our senses, and for the shutting out of any chance of learning to read and write like children of our age in other employments.

We respect our masters, and are willing to work for our support, and that of our parents and brothers; but we want time for more rest, a little play, and to learn to read and write. Young as we are, we find that we could do our work better if we were to work less time, and were not so weighed down by the long continuance of our daily toil.

We do not think it right that we should know nothing but work and suffering, from Monday morning to Saturday night, to make others rich.

Do, good gentlemen, inquire into our condition. Let not a respect for wealth disguise from your view our severe wrongs, nor restrain you from declaring what measure of justice is due to us. Indeed, we tell you no lies, when we say that our bodies are wasted, and our strength sinking, under our daily tasks; and that we are without any time for amusement or learning. Surely the King does not intend that his youngest subjects should be worked the hardest and suffer the most.

We throw ourselves upon your mercy and justice. Look at us, and say if it is possible that we can be disbelieved. Do your duty faithfully to us. Tell the King the actual state in which you find us. So shall you cause relief to come from our rulers; and so you will be repaid by good wishes from the grateful hearts of thousands of little children like ourselves.

The Bill was finally passed, and at the same time the first factory inspectors were appointed.

Inevitably, there were some who found the "satanic mills" inspiring. A certain John Jones wrote this hymn of praise in 1821:

Now see the Cotton from the town convey'd
To Manchester, that glorious mart of trade;
Hail splendid scene! The Nurse of every art,
That glads the widow's and the orphan's heart!
Thy mills, like gorgeous palaces arise,
And lift their useful turrets to the skies!
See Kennedy's stupendous structure join'd
To thine M'Connell-friends of human kind!
Whose ready doors for ever expand

To give employment to a numerous band.
Murray's behold! that well deserves a name,—
And Lee's and Houldsworth's our attention claim—
And numerous others, scattered up and down,
The sole supporters of this ample town.

9

NO MUCK—NO BRASS

An old map of the mid-nineteenth century designates the number and position of the cotton mills by black dots along the Irwell from its upper reaches down towards the confluence with the Mersey. Not only along the river itself do the dots cluster, but many are shown also along the banks of the numerous brooks which flow into it. There is the Bradshaw, Hollins, Cheesden, Tottington, Naden, Whitwell Greaves, Swinnel and several others, including some that are long enough to have earned for themselves the title of river: the Roch, the Tonge, Croal and Irk.

Life was hard enough for the people of the mills along these waterways, but it was even harder when the mills were silent, the tall chimneys smokeless; and the time of tragedy came in 1860 when, far away across the Atlantic, the guns of Fort Sumter signalled the start of the American Civil War. By 1861 the Northern fleet was blockading Confederate ports and the cotton on which Lancashire depended was no longer coming. The Liverpool docks were quiet, and the mills along the Irwell and its tributaries ground to a halt.

Many refused to believe that the American war could last for long; but the few months' stock of cotton held in the warehouses ran out and there was no sign of the end. For a while the savings banks and the loan funds of co-operative societies kept a lot of workers going; then thousands began to petition the Board of Guardians for bread. Relief committees were set up, though Manchester lagged behind other towns in this.

There was still a supply of Indian cotton, but it was of a very inferior quality to that grown on the slave plantations of the American South. It broke frequently and needed expensive alteration of machinery to handle it.

Public meetings were held, in the Free Trade Hall and other places. Some urged recognition of the Southern Confederacy by Britain, and the use of British warships to convoy the cargoes of cotton across the Atlantic. Others declared that such cotton would be "stained with blood, cursed with the support of slavery". The topicality of Harriet Beecher Stowe's *Uncle Tom's Cabin* made it a best seller.

Sewing classes were organized to repair old clothes donated by people all over Britain. Crime was stated not to have risen above average, but prostitution—which the Victorians usually preferred to believe did not exist—was admitted to show a rise. In 1861 there were in Manchester 5,408 illegitimate births; in 1862, 5,707;

and in 1863, 5,735. Such comparatively small increases were probably only the tip of an iceberg of such births, most of which never found their way on to official records.

One Relief Committee secured a grant of £200 with which to "assist suffering resulting from immoral conduct". This was denounced by ardent Christian gentlemen as a "bastardy promotion fund".

Relief was given out by the Board of Guardians on the basis of food tickets worth 3*s.* each. An able-bodied man could have one ticket every three days; a man with wife and two children 6*s.* for six days. Sometimes there would be a free issue of clogs and these would be almost as gratefully received as the food tickets. Footwear was expensive and the alternative was to wrap one's feet in sacking.

A song written about 1863 includes the following verse:

> O dear! Iv yon Yankees could nobbut just see,
> Heaw they're clemmin' an' starvin' poor weavers loike me,
> Aw think they'd soon sattle their bother, an' strive
> To send us some cotton to keep us alive.

In 1862 the writer Edwin Waugh toured the area and wrote of his impressions in the *Manchester Examiner and Times.* He found that, although the poor depended on the Guardians for survival, the authorities were not exactly popular. As one recipient of meal tickets commented to Mr. Waugh, "Thim Guardians is the awfullest set of min in the world! A man had better be transported than come under 'em".

Shopkeepers had little alternative but to allow as much credit as possible in the hope of being paid eventually. As one said, "Win a deel o' brass owin', but it's mostly owin' by folk as'll pay sometime".

Mr. Waugh describes a visit to one family:

> We turned into a low, narrow entry, very dark and damp. Two more turns brought us to a dirty, pent-up corner, where a low door stood open. We entered. It was a cold, gloomy-looking hovel scarcely three yards square. There was no fire in the little rusty grate. The day was sunny but no sunshine could ever reach that nook, nor any fresh breezes disturb the pestilent vapours that harboured there, festering in the sluggish gloom. In one corner of the place a little worn and broken stair led up to a room of the same size above where, I was told, there was some straw for the family to sleep on. But the only furniture in the house was a little broken deal table, reared up against the stairs because one leg was gone, and two rickety chairs.

Just round the corner Mr. Waugh stopped at the open door of a very small cottage. A good-looking young Irishwoman sat there, upon a three-legged stool, suckling her child. She was clean, and had an intelligent look.

"What do you pay for this nook?" she was asked.

The Crescent, Salford, 1967. *Salford Local History Library*

Broughton Suspension Bridge, Lower Broughton. *Salford Local History Library*

"We pay eightpence a week—and they *will* have it, my word!"

Mr. Waugh asked, "What income do you have now?"

"We have eightpence a head in the week, an' the rent to pay out o' that, or else they'll turn us out."

Another family encountered in the peregrinations of Mr. Waugh was four in number: man, wife and two children. The husband used to earn not more than 7*s.* per week at the loom. Now they were not receiving any relief because, the wife explained, when her husband

> ". . . had bin eawt o' work a good while he turn't his hond to shavin'. But it brings varra little in—we hev to trust so much. He shaves four on 'em for a hawpenny, an' there's a deal on 'em cannot pay that. Then they cannot for shame to come, so we lose'n their custom till sich times as summat turns up at they can raise a trifle to pay up wi'."

The next visit was to an Irish family. There was an old woman and a flaxen-haired lad about ten years of age. She was sitting on the only chair in the place, and the tattered lad was kneeling on the ground before her while she combed his hair.

The tireless Mr. Waugh walked the cramped streets during 1862 and 1863, and the snatches of conversation from his account of visits to the cottages and tenements of the unemployed are vivid glimpses of the misery caused by this breakdown in the new industrial life that had brought the previous generation from the land to the cities.

"... We are five altogether in this house ... this lass is a weaver reeler, I am a weaver; but we'n bin out o' wark nine months now. We'n bin force't to tak to relief at last; an we'n getten five tickets. We could happen ha' manage't better—but aw'm sore wi' rheumatism, yo see'n ... "

" ... I made application for th' watchman's place at Leyland Mill, but I wur too late. ... There's a woman i'th next street at's gettin' four tickets fro th' relief folk, reggilar, an' her husban's addlin' thirty shillin' a week o' time as a sinker. Aw consider such wark as that's noan reet. ... My daughter has been eawt o' wark a long time. I can make about two shillin' an' sixpence a week; but we've three shillin' a week to pay for rent, an we must pay it, too, or else turn out."

Many of the unemployed took to the streets as wandering minstrels. It became common to see little groups of "shy, sad-looking singers and instrumentalists performing in the work-worn clothing of factory operatives". The folk arts of singing and making one's own music, even composing, were still alive among the factory workers. The industrial life had not yet had time to kill such arts as it has since; and these talents responded to the crisis. A number of "songs of distress" were written and sung by the wandering minstrels in the streets of the cotton towns. The following song was one that became very popular. The verses were also printed on cards and sold at railway stations in aid of the Relief Fund. Its title was "The Smokeless Chimney".

Stranger! Who to buy art willing,
Seek not here for talent rare:
Mine's no song of love or beauty,
But a tale of want and care.

Traveller on the Northern Railway!
Look and learn, as on you speed;
See the hundred smokeless chimneys,
Learn their tale of cheerless need.

Ah! Perchance the landscape fairer
Charms your taste, your artist-eye;
Little do you guess how dearly
Costs that now unclouded sky.

"How much prettier is this country!"
Says the careless passer-by.
"Clouds of smoke we see no longer.
What's the reason?—Tell me why."

"Better far it were, most surely,
Never more such clouds to see,
Bringing taint o'er nature's beauty,
With their foul obscurity."

Thoughtless fair one! From yon chimney
    Floats the golden breath of life.
Stop that current at your pleasure!
    Stop! and starve the child,—the wife!

Ah! To them each smokeless chimney
    Is a signal of despair,
They see hunger, sickness, ruin,
    Written in that pure, bright air.

"Mother! Mother! See! 'Twas truly
    Said last week the mill would stop!
Mark yon chimney,—nought is going,—
    There's no smoke from out o'th top!"

"The Smokeless Chimney" has more verses, but the last one sums up the dismal truth of the old Lancashire saying that "where there's muck there's brass". Only in recent times have we begun to realize that you *can* have the brass without the muck.

Pray that Peace soon bringing
    Work and plenty in her train,
We may see these smokeless chimneys
    Blackening all the land again.

Another song, written by the "Blackburn Bard" runs:

The time will come, as come again it must
When Lancashire shall lift her head once more;

Her suffering sons, now down amid the dust
Of indigence, shall pass through Plenty's door;
Her commerce cover seas from shore to shore;
Her arts arise to highest eminence;
Her products prove unrivall'd, as of yore;
Her valor and her virtue—men of sense,
And blue-eyed beauties,—England's pride and her
    defence.

The great conflict raging on a faraway continent finally came to its end. The Confederacy surrendered; the way of life on the Southern plantations was "gone with the wind", and the slaves were—officially, anyway—freed.

In the summer of 1864 there were jubilant, even tearful, scenes as the first wagonloads of cotton began to arrive again from Liverpool. Union Jacks, the emblems of various friendly societies, even shawls, were hung from the windows of houses. Preceded by musicians, scores of men and women hastened to railway sidings and pushed the welcome wagons into the mill-yards.

The looms roared into life, smoke belched again from the tall chimneys, rubbish spewed forth into the Irwell—and once again there was "brass" in the pockets of the factory folk.

10

THE IRWELL'S OTHER INDUSTRIES

Cotton was the first major product of the Industrial Revolution, and its mills the first to pollute on any significant scale the clear waters of that sweet river which Julius Agricola and his legion had found. There are, however, traces of industrial activity which preceded not only cotton and the steam engine but even water power itself. Iron was mined on a small scale in South Lancashire in the thirteenth century. In the 1870s the remains of four "bloomeries" were discovered in the Rossendale area, one of them about three miles from the source of the Irwell.

A bloomerie was a primitive furnace in which the iron ore was covered with stones and clay beneath which it was heated, the necessary draught being provided by the ingenius method of establishing the bloomerie on a hill facing the prevailing wind, and on those exposed heights of the Irwell's birthplace a wind was rarely lacking. On the occasional days when the wind ceased to blow a bellows was employed, operated either by hand or by foot. Much arduous hammering and constant reheating was necessary to remove some of the impurities from the crude ore.

Quite probably some of the iron would have been carried by pack-horses downstream to where the Irwell became navigable and then shipped on rafts or in boats propelled by oars down to the Mersey and the coastal towns. Certainly the iron was used in Warrington which became a famous centre for the manufacture of nails, tools and wire.

Lead was also mined in Rossendale in the Middle Ages, and some mines have been found at Thieveley Pike north of Bacup, dating even from as recently as the seventeenth century. There are also traces of lead mining on Anglezark Moor near to Limestone Brook.

The cotton mills began to arrive on the Irwell during the 1780s, and were followed soon afterwards by small engineering factories along the banks of the Irwell, Medlock, Irk and some of the brooks in the hills. In those early years they all needed the force of running water as a power source and since this was free and plentiful the factories were able to make castings, boilers, iron girders and, most important of all, more waterwheels. By the 1830s steam power was well established and the waterwheels no longer needed. Now the factories were making textile machinery, engines and even locomotives for the new railways. With the decline of water power the hill streams where cotton was still king could be abandoned. More and more of the new factories were then built along the low reaches of the river where they were able to use the waterway for transport to the Mersey and also pour into it all their waste products.

Even bridges were being made by the middle of the nineteenth century as the flood tide of the Industrial Revolution gathered momentum and the roaring factories spewed forth their cornucopia of new inventions. A road bridge which still spans the Medlock at Albion Street was made in the Knott Mill Ironworks founded by John Gallow, a Scot born in Manchester following the arrival of his father who in 1790 started the Caledonian Foundry in Great Bridgewater Street. Besides the Albion Street bridge John Gallow made some of the first locomotives for the Liverpool and Manchester Railway.

At Worsley the Mesnes Ironworks specialized in colliery equipment, some of which, made in the nineteenth century, is still in use in Lancashire pits.

In 1846 on the Salford side of the river, near Chapel Street and the Victoria Bridge, two engineers, William and Colin Mather took over an ironworks. The firm they created eventually became the well-known Mather and Platt Ltd. One of their greatest triumphs was the production of an early type of steamship which was sailed down the Irwell, along the Mersey to Liverpool and thence across to the Isle of Man, despite the prophecies of experts that it was bound to sink on the way. The company later moved from the Irwell to a bigger site in the Newton Heath district of North Manchester where they produced sprinkler systems, a revolutionary new method of putting out fires which established the fame of Mather and Platt in the realm of fire-fighting. Sprinklers can be seen today in the ceilings of most modern buildings and ocean liners.

Paper-making was one of the earliest of industries to come to the river. The manufacture of paper requires a plentiful supply of water and most of the mills were built in the Irwell Valley and along the Croal. There were also two at Throstle Nest, just past the site of Pomona Gardens, but these disappeared with the coming of the Ship Canal. Rags and various other raw materials needed in paper manufacture were pounded into pulp by stamping machines which were at first water-powered. Later came a steam-driven stamper invented in Holland and known as the Hollander. One of the most well-known paper manufacturers was the East Lancashire Paper Mill Co. Ltd., established in 1860. With the opening of the Ship Canal this concern and others profited immensely by the importation of wood-pulp from Scandinavia and North America.

The development of the 1200-acre industrial estate of Trafford Park followed naturally on the construction of the Manchester Ship Canal which incorporates the Irwell from Throstle Nest onwards. Some means of rescuing Manchester from its transport problems had become a vital necessity by the early 1880s. Barge traffic on the Irwell and Mersey route to the coast, or along the Bridgewater Canal to Runcorn on the Mersey estuary, was incapable of coping with more than a tiny fraction of the products from the vast industrial conurbation which had arisen from those first water-powered cotton mills. Even the Liverpool and Manchester Railway was inadequate, and goods traffic by road did not exist in Victorian England, the internal combustion engine being still only a gleam in the eye of German inventor Gottlieb Daimler.

The Ship Canal was opened in 1894, and saved Manchester from commercial extinction, as the cost of transporting goods from Manchester to Liverpool was as much as shipping them across the Atlantic. A great growth of industry came with the Canal, like a second Industrial Revolution.

It became obvious that ships would require repairs, and the Manchester Dry Docks Co. Ltd. was founded for this purpose. The company also built steel dumb barges of up to 700 tons deadweight.

In 1907 advertisements designed to attract firms to what was by then one of Europe's largest and most modern concentrations of technologically advanced industry, described it in ecstatic terms. One such example of early twentieth-century advertiser's prose announced Trafford Park as "An American corner of old jog-trot England"!

American firms had been quick to seize the opportunity. In 1901 George Westinghouse had established in the Park a factory for the production of power station equipment which eventually became the great GEC/AEI complex, employing about 25,000 workers at its peak in the affluent 1960s, although more recently redundancies and Britain's declining economy have reduced the plant to a shadow of its former self. Westinghouse was followed by Henry Ford who built the first car assembly shops in Britain, removed from the Park to Dagenham in 1925.

In the 1830s John Nasmyth (1808–90) established the Bridgewater Foundry in the district of Eccles on a site conveniently close to the Bridgewater Canal and the Liverpool and Manchester Railway line. Nasmyth, besides being an engineer of genius, was also an artist and amateur astronomer. He observed the stars with a ten-inch reflecting telescope in the gardens of his house in Patricroft and his imaginative drawings of lunar landscapes were shown at the Great Exhibition in Hyde Park in 1851. His design for the Nelson monument in Trafalgar Square was at one stage accepted by the organizing committee, being rejected later only because its cost would have exceeded the budget available.

The Bridgewater Foundry was planned on mass-production lines that were considerably ahead of its time, with a railway and cranes running through the workshops. It was also constructed in such a manner that it could be transformed into a cotton mill should the engineering business fail.

Nasmyth made steam engines, hydraulic presses and pumps. Two of his original machines, the design of which represented great advance in their time, are now preserved in the Monks Hall Museum in Eccles. A six-ton steam hammer, invented by this Da Vinci of the nineteenth century, was said to have been so delicately balanced that it could crack an egg on top of a wineglass without damaging the glass.

In 1838 a locomotive was built in the foundry and was named—appropriately—"The Bridgewater". Nasmyth gave it a trial run on the Liverpool and Manchester line without first obtaining top-level permission. During the run a senior official was encountered who expressed severe disapproval at the sight of an unauthorized engine "on our railway". In a letter of explanation to the Company afterwards Nasmyth commented that "We fell in with a disabled train and returned with it to Manchester".

Ceramics was another industry which grew rapidly during the nineteenth century. The Pilkington Tile and Pottery Co. Ltd. produced the famous Lancastrian Pottery in the factory on the Irwell near Prestolee.

As industry expanded so the strength of the organized worker also increased, the various unions joining together in 1864 to form the TUC. Gladstone's Act of 1871 ensured the right to strike and Disraeli's Act of 1875 legalized "peaceful picketing".

There were many strikes as workers fought to reduce their hours of work, increase their pay and enforce legislation against dangerous machinery and contamination by the many new chemical processes.

There was no Welfare State in those days to cushion the grimness of life without pay during a strike, but even so there were times when the employers found that victory after a prolonged struggle could be more costly than surrender. Well might an exasperated employer have said in the 1890s when faced with a demand for fewer hours and better conditions, "Give in to this and they'll be wanting cups of tea at their benches next!"

In the early decades of the nineteenth century the owners of the new industries often built their homes along pleasant stretches of the Irwell or its tributaries, but increasing pollution from their own factories gradually forced them to retreat into outlying villages such as Gatley, Cheadle and Bramhall. Few of them had any concern for the mess that they were leaving for the twentieth century to clean up.

11

SOME IRWELLIAN CHARACTERS

The Irwell boasts many characters in its long history, but perhaps the strangest of all was Ann Lee, who sailed the river in a boat manned by a crew of ardent disciples who believed her to be Christ reborn in female form.

Born on February 29, 1736, in Toad Lane (now Todd Street), close to Manchester Cathedral and the river, Ann Lee, high priestess of the religion of Shakerism, was destined to find the smoky air of the eighteenth century cotton town too stifling for her religious fervour. In an age of theological orthodoxy the blacksmith's daughter chose to be different.

As soon as she was old enough Ann went to work as a cutter of hatter's fur, and then as cook at Manchester Infirmary which stood in what is now Piccadilly Gardens. Serious, thoughtful, she lacked the joyousness of normal children and, in fact, tended to frighten them with her talk of being favoured by visions.

In 1758 she joined the Shakers, a small remnant of a

group of "French Prophets" who came to England in 1706. When Ann became a member they numbered about thirty and were led by Jane and James Wardley, two former Quakers. According to Shaker belief, Jane Wardley was the spirit of John the Baptist reborn to prepare the way for the Second Coming of Christ who was also to return as a woman.

The Shaker movement had already attracted attention because of the wild and frenzied dancing in which the participants worked themselves into a condition of high hysteria.

Ann, an illiterate but with an obviously magnetic personality, described as being of medium height, with blue eyes and chestnut hair, soon began to exercise a powerful influence upon the Shakers who were earnestly looking for some sign of the Second Coming.

Determined to spread her mission far and wide, Ann and her little band hired a boat—there are no records as to the type of vessel—and for some months in the summer of 1769 they sailed to and fro along the length of the river, calling frequently at small villages to hold public meetings, and sometimes give exhibitions of their extraordinary dancing. The following year Ann was imprisoned for "sabbath-breaking, dancing, shouting, shaking and performing other extremes of religious behaviour in the street".

Shortly after her release she became officially head of the Shakers. She was arrested again in 1771, on this occasion at a meeting where she was preaching against the temptations of the flesh. She was sent to Bedlam as being of unsound mind, but was released within a few weeks.

Despairing at last of ever converting the indifferent Mancunians, Ann led her chosen people out of the wilderness that was Lancashire to the promised land across the ocean. On May 19, 1774, she and about a dozen Shakers sailed for America where they were to found a number of thriving religious colonies.

* * *

Murder on New Bailey Bridge—murder on a night of freezing mist that hangs low and menacing over the frozen river. The year is 1813, the month December, and a flow of sub-zero air from Siberia holds England in a grip of ice the severity of which has not been known in living memory.

In the south the Thames is frozen solid, and fairs are held on its glassy surface. The whole of Europe is in the same fierce grip, although in France the allied armies slog through the winter, closing the net on Napoleon beleaguered in Paris.

In Lancashire the temperature is not quite as low as in the south, and the ice on the Irwell not quite thick enough for a fair, but the fog makes conditions less pleasant than along the Thames.

On the night of December 17 a young woman emerges from a house in Bridge Street and begins walking towards the bridge—and her destiny.

Her name is Lavinia Robinson, and according to a

Kersall Bend.

Salford Local History Library

The Irwell, looking east from Broughton Bridge. Strangeways Prison tower Salford Local History Library

description which is later to be placed in the local press, she is "about 30 years of age and of good figure, of a fair complexion with long light brown hair. She had a fawn coloured coat, a pink and yellow shot figured kerchief on her neck, a black beaver cottage bonnet and her linen was marked L.R."

Lavinia—schoolmistress—was burdened with the title of spinster, a shameful title for a nineteenth-century miss approaching thirty. Lavinia has had at least one suitor from whom she parted only a few months ago, and now she is engaged to John, a good-looking young surgeon with prospects and an address in the same street.

The course of love, however, has not been running smoothly. The previous evening John had taxed her with seeing again the man who had earlier held her affections. In Lavinia's house the two had quarrelled bitterly, the quarrel continuing into the street to the entertainment of the neighbours.

Lavinia has told her father that she is going to meet John to patch things up. In 1813 young women do not usually go walking abroad alone at night, but Lavinia is a strong-willed individual, accustomed to doing things on her own to a greater extent than most of her sex, and her father has long since learned the futility of opposing her.

She nears the bridge, the frosty air magnifying the tap of her heels on the stone cobbles of the narrow streets. Who has asked for this meeting? Lavinia? John? We shall never know. Neither shall we know what happened on the bridge that cold night. We know only that John is there, waiting in the gloom of the bridge. He admits it later.

"She threw her arms round my neck and begged me to believe that she had no longer any association with this other man," John will say when questioned. "But I did not believe her. I pushed her arms aside and I walked away. I did not see her again."

There is no one to observe this fatal meeting, but Lavinia does not return home. By morning the family are alarmed. There is no police station to go to in the early nineteenth century, so her father inserts an advertisement in the local newspaper, offering a reward of thirty guineas.

Someone suggests dragging the river, but now the weather has become even colder and the ice too thick to break and so it remains for many weeks.

On the morning of February 7, 1814, a Mr Goodier, of Mode Wheel, is walking by the river bank when he sees Lavinia, floating near to the side, encased and perfectly preserved in a coffin-like block of slowly-melting ice. Her head is actually protruding from one end of the block, and the frozen crystals entangled in her hair give the appearance of a bridal coronet.

And so Lavinia came back, floating, as Mr Goodier picturesquely phrased it "like Ophelia on the Irwell".

A newspaper described the finding of Lavinia in the romantic terms favoured by journalists of the day: "This ill-starred maiden reclining on a sandbank environed by masses of ice with icicles gemming her hair in place of orange blossoms. Decay had scarcely touched her loveliness with his effacing finger . . . "

There were no marks of violence on her body, and in 1814 no forensic scientists to carry out a detailed examination, but neighbours had no doubt about the cause of her death. A mob broke the windows of the young surgeon's house, he was insulted in the street, and for his own safety he fled the district.

Thousands attended the funeral of the "Manchester Ophelia" when Lavinia was laid to rest in St. John's Churchyard with the following inscription on her gravestone:

> More lasting than in lines of art
> Thy spoiled character imprest,
> Thy worth engraved on every heart,
> Thy loss bewailed in every breast.

* * *

Another well-known personality of the nineteenth century was Sam Scott. In newspaper cuttings and various personal "reminiscences" there are occasional mentions of this curious American character who, for some inexplicable reason, liked to jump into rivers. Even in those days the best sort of publicity was to have a gimmick, and river-jumping was Sam Scott's particular speciality.

Information about him is very scanty. There are

just brief tantalizing notes about "The Jumper" who arrived in Manchester from America in 1837 and attracted attention—and some money—by his spectacular leaps into the Irwell which in that year was still reasonably clean.

In December of that year Sam announced that he would jump from a five-storey warehouse near the New Bailey Bridge. Watched by a huge crowd he appeared on the roof "attired in lace drawers, a red flannel shirt and a bladder drawn over the scalp". He ran over the slates and, after addressing the spectators and expressing the hope that they would give of their money generously, he sprang into the river.

A local newspaper reported the scene:

> He presented an erect position during the time he was in the air, with his legs and arms slightly separated from each other. When he came to the surface he had clenched in his hands some small stones that he had grasped from the bottom. The river was swollen by rain but was no more than twelve feet deep.

Sam Scott departed from the Irwell as mysteriously as he had come, but in the book *Lancashire, the First Industrial Society,* by C. Aspin, there appears the intriguing statement that he was "accidentally hanged on Waterloo Bridge, London, in January, 1841".

* * *

In 1889 the Irwell took Mark Addy, perhaps in vengeance because, in the course of his life, he snatched no fewer than fifty-five persons from its watery, chemical-sodden grasp.

Mark was born in 1838 in a curious, Italianate-style tenement in the Parsonage, near Blackfriars Bridge, known as the Stage Buildings. His father owned various pleasure boats and racing craft for hire on the river, and Mark grew up by the water, unafraid of the swirling current.

He learnt to swim at Greengate Baths, but in fact had already saved two lives even before he could swim—one by floating on a plank alongside a struggling man and the other by wading into the water up to his neck.

When he grew up Mark married and acquired a tavern on the Salford side of the river, and whenever anyone was seen to be in difficulties the cry would go up, "Bring Mark Addy!" Mark would abandon his customers and race to the water, another life to save.

He won a number of medals, including the Gold Medal and the Silver Medal of the Humane Society for the Hundred of Salford and then the Bronze Medal of the Royal Humane Society; but the real accolade came with the award of the Albert Medal, First Class, which was presented by the Mayor of Salford, Alderman Robinson, in the large Assembly Room of the Town Hall in Bexley Square. in 1878.

His Worship, who seems to have regarded the occasion as a useful exercise for his own voice, opened the proceedings by explaining that

> . . . it had occurred to him that the most fitting thing to do would be to assemble the inhabitants at a public meeting in order that they might do honour to Mark Addy on the occasion of the presentation (cheers for this brilliant inspiration). Mark Addy's exploits of daring and bravery on the River Irwell had extended over a period of twenty-five or twenty-six years during which time he had been successful in saving forty of his fellow creatures (loud applause) frequently at the imminent risk of his own life (cheers). The first instance occurred when Addy was only fourteen years of age, at which time he could not swim. Since then he had acquired the art of swimming at Greengate Baths. (Hear, Hear.)

According to the account in the *Salford Reporter* the Mayor then droned on for several minutes, not about Mark Addy but on the history of the Albert Medal itself. Towards the end of this discourse his Worship observed that

> There is provision for recalling the medal in the case of misconduct on the part of the recipient; but (he assured his audience) in Addy's case I am certain that this will be a dead letter (cheers).

Turning to our hero the Mayor continued:

> I hope you will live many years to come and that you will wear this medal, not only as high mark of your

past services, but that it will be to you an incentive to further efforts (applause).

The police band played "God Save the Queen", and three cheers were dutifully given for Her Majesty; then with another three for the guest of honour, Colonel W. H. Walker, M.P., the proceedings ended.

Mark was accompanied by the Mayoral party to a carriage and pair outside in the Square where a crowd cheered wildly and the police band obliged with a rendering of "See the Conquering Hero Comes".

That same hero was to continue snatching souls from the Irwell for another eleven years—until the fatal Whit Monday in 1889. For fifty-one years the river had put up with Mark Addy and his rescues, and the river had waited with patient certainty. It had seen so many brief-lived mortals that it could afford to wait. Early Britons, Romans, Vikings, Saxons, Normans, all had been claimed in their turn, drinking its waters into their lungs; and now this impudent creature thought he could go on depriving the river of its destined prey.

In the afternoon a boy fell into the water at Factory Lane, and Mark was called, and he saved the boy. It is said that he swallowed a few mouthfuls of Irwell, which, years before, in Mark's youth, would not have mattered.

In 1889 what Mark imbibed was a complex chemical formula brewed in scores of mills and factories. Already suffering ill health, Mark was soon taken to his bed, never to recover.

His memory is perpetuated in several forms. There is a large memorial to him in Weaste Cemetery where he was buried; there is the Mark Addy Award, a swimming trophy which is still given; and at Woden Street, between Pomona Docks and Regent Road, is the little known Mark Addy Footbridge. In the Art Gallery in Salford's Peel Park there hangs a portrait in oils showing Mark wearing his medals.

* * *

Castle Irwell, which stood on a rise of ground overlooking the river where it flows through Broughton, once housed another character who deserves to be included in the "Irwellian" classification. This was John Perceval Fitzgerald, brother of the more famous—and less eccentric—Edward Fitzgerald who translated the *Rubá'iyát* of Omar Khayyám into English in 1859.

John Perceval was a religious devotee who spent much of his time delivering tracts to his neighbours' houses and, in his more excitable moods, vocally accosting in the street those who were not quick enough to dart down the nearest escape route.

In church he had the disturbing habit of removing his boots and stockings and spreading the contents of his pockets on the pew seats so that he could settle down in comfort. He was often a distraction to the minister for he would frequently give vent to a shrill whistle if the sermon did not find favour with him; and not many sermons succeeded in so doing.

Anyone unwise enough to invite him to take the chair at a meeting soon regretted it, for his address was liable to last a whole evening and would be either about religion or temperance. On such occasions his disrobing performance went to even greater lengths than when he was in church.

* * *

In the early years of the eighteenth century a young man might sometimes have been seen standing on the banks of the Irwell at a spot near Agecroft Bridge. He would be declaiming in Latin the orations of Tully, or perhaps those of the silver-tongued Cicero. Long, wavy hair blowing in the summer breeze, this good-looking youth would have an admiring audience of one—his sister Sarah. Her love for her gifted brother was such that when he wanted a new wig, her father had written: "Let us know whether you will have it a natural one. When you have we will venture it, and so you may be sure of your sister's good hair and no cheet."

John Byrom (1692–1763), who wrote the hymn "Christians Awake", was an accomplished linguist, fluent in the Latin in which he wrote numerous letters and poems to friends, reading Greek easily, speaking French and Italian; he also learnt German for the sole pleasure of being able to read in the original the works of a mystical philosopher named Boehm to whose theories he was addicted. He was also a lifelong student of Hebrew. His life in the family home called Kersal

Cell, a bare thirty yards from the Irwell, was that of an educated man of independent means, free to indulge his literary talents as he wished. He believed that "Take time enough; all other graces will soon fill up their proper places". Across the years his life and character have an appeal which is far greater than that of other and more flamboyant characters who have stormed their way through the pages of history. He lived just before the Industrial Revolution, before the smoke of the chimneys darkened the skies, before the engines roared and the stench of pollution came to the clear waters of the Irwell.

Byrom spent his days strolling through the wooded cloughs of the Irwell Valley, rowing leisurely on the river, composing poetry in his study bedroom overlooking a grove of yew trees which stood between house and river, studying the great philosophers in English, Latin, Greek; writing lengthy letters to his numerous friends on the topics of the day or debating abstruse questions of philosophy.

He began his education at a school in Chester, then went to the Merchant Taylors' in London from which he graduated to Trinity, Cambridge in 1709, where he became a close friend of a nephew of Richard Bentley, Master of Trinity, and through him was inspired by Bentley's eleven-year-old daughter Joanna to write his *Colin and Phoebe,* published in the *Spectator* on October 6, 1714. Though almost forgotten today this work was described at the time as "one of the most exquisite examples of playful poetry".

After leaving Cambridge Byrom dallied with the study of physics and went to France where he stayed for a year at Montpellier, which gave him the opportunity of perfecting his French.

On his return to England he married his cousin Elizabeth and shortly afterwards settled down to invent a system of shorthand. Although the eighteenth century was not an age of reportage, students often resorted to some form of abbreviation to reduce the tedium and the time-consuming task of writing lengthy works and translations by hand. Cypher writing had been in vogue for some time, and Pepys had used it in his Diaries.

Byrom's shorthand was the parent of all later forms, being the first to be founded on a definite principle, but the use of shorthand did have its dangers. Byrom went to take notes at a sermon being given by a fiery orator named Horley who abruptly broke off his discourse and objected to being reported on the grounds that his words "might be used against me". He threatened to turn out the "chiel amang them takin' notes". Byrom refused to leave, even when he was offered the return of the 1*s*. entry fee which he had paid. Horley then proceeded to gabble the rest of his sermon at a furious pace in the hope that he would be too fast to be taken down, with the result that he was also too fast for most of his audience to understand him.

There is a story that in 1744 Charles Stuart the Pretender had slipped incognito into Lancashire and stayed for a night as guest at Kersal Cell. As there is no proof of this it is almost certainly one of those myths with which history's pages are liberally scattered. Nevertheless, Byrom did develop Jacobite leanings, and was always ready to use his pen in the cause of the Pretender. It was known that he had met the Pretender while in France and had kissed his hand at Avignon.

His daughter Beppy, when she grew up, was an ardent Jacobite; although James Croston, in his *Nooks and Corners of Lancashire and Cheshire* (1882), comments:

> The gossiping daughter was an arrant Jacobite, though a prudent one; her devotion to the Stuart cause being most pronounced when danger was remote.

In 1745, when the Pretender entered Manchester with his Scottish supporters and camped in St. Ann's Square, Beppy made her one politically incautious move and putting on her best white dress she went into town for the thrill of kissing the Pretender's hand. Both she and her father were staying at the time in their small town house in Hanging Ditch, but they suddenly took fright and retreated to Kersal Cell, while the Pretender rode south to his destiny, his English followers soon melting away like snowflakes.

Shortly afterwards Byrom wrote:

> The Stuart cause, leaning on the Scott,
> Pierced to the very centre of the realm,
> In hope to seize his abdicated helm.

The Byroms were fortunate in escaping the vengeance that fell upon many who had welcomed the Pretender. Some of their neighbours had their windows broken and were personally molested by mobs of angry loyalists. Some of the more well-known Jacobites were imprisoned for treasonable activities and a few were executed.

John Byrom settled down again to his quiet rural life. He died in 1763, easily and without suffering, an end in keeping with the civilized tenor of a life that had flowed as evenly as the river by his home.

* * *

A curious development among the mill workers along the Irwell was the rise of many amateur botanical societies, often founded by self-educated men, struggling to learn to read and write at the Mechanic's Institutes after a long day in the mill.

Despite their long hours of work these worthy students found time for amateur scientific pursuits. They acquired small libraries for their societies and sometimes raised as many as two hundred members to attend annual meetings of district associations.

A clog-maker named Buxton, who sold Sunday newspapers to supplement his meagre income, wrote a very useful botanical guide which was published in 1849. When over sixty years of age Buxton would walk over twenty-five miles a day through the wooded cloughs of the Irwell Valley, or over the wild uplands of Millstone Grit, in search of plants for his collection. In his book he comments that "Fields and woods, although the rich man's heritage, may still be the poor man's flower garden."

Another of them, James Crowther, would set off after a long day's work in search of a specimen of which he'd heard. He would walk up to twenty miles or more, returning in the middle of the night for a brief sleep before rising in time to be back at the mill.

Mrs. Gaskell, in her work *Mary Barton,* published in 1848, referred to these working-class students of science:

> There is a class of men in Manchester, unknown even to many of the inhabitants, and whose existence will probably be doubted by many, who yet may claim kindred with all the noble names that science recognizes. I said "in Manchester", but they are scattered all over the manufacturing districts of Lancashire. In the neighbourhood of Oldham there are weavers, common hand-loom weavers, who throw the shuttle with unceasing sound, though Newton's *Principia* lie open on the loom, to be snatched at in working hours, but revelled over in meal times or at night. It is perhaps less astonishing that the more popularly interesting branches of natural history have their warm and devoted followers among this class. There are botanists among them, equally familiar with either the Linnaean or the Natural system, who know the name and habitat of every plant within a day's walk from their dwellings, who steal a day or two when any particular plant should be in flower,

and tying up their simple food in their pocket handkerchiefs, set off to fetch home the humble-looking weed. There are entomologists who may be seen with a rude-looking net, ready to catch any winged insect, or a kind of dredge with which they rake the green and slimy pools; practical, shrewd, hard-working men, who pore over every new specimen with real scientific delight.

* * *

Such were a few of the outstanding personalities who lived and died in the communities along the Irwell.

12

PLEASURE DAYS

Many generations of early Britons drank the sweet waters of the Irwell, probably ducked their lice-infested heads in the cleansing flow whenever the irritation became too great; used shallow sections near the banks as public conveniences. Centuries later these places were known in the Anglo-Saxon language as "shitters", a word which became impolite only in comparatively recent times when we took to relieving ourselves in private and so came to regard any word associated with the excretory functions as obscene.

Most of all, however, the Irwell has been used as a source of food. For more than two thousand years it has yielded gudgeon, chubb, salmon, eels and several other finny delicacies. The Celts sold their catches to the Roman occupiers and later to the Danes. Then came the Norman overlords who established the rights of private ownership over fishing.

In the nineteenth century when the entire world was

The confluence of the Irwell (on the left) and the Mersey, from a photograph taken early this century.

A contemporary print of the Manchester and Salford regatta, 1844, showing on the right fields, farm buildings and a grandstand where Manchester Docks now are.

Victoria Bridge from Blackfriars Bridge, 1859. The Cathedral tower is *Salford Local History Library*

changed and the destiny of humanity affected by the Industrial Revolution, the fish of the Irwell were among the first casualties of that upheaval which caused the pollution of the environment to which we are only now really awakening.

In the nineteenth century there were still some private fishing grounds: for example, the Manchester Hotel, with gardens sloping down to the Irk near to its junction with the Irwell, owned a permit to fish for salmon. The hotel was also the residence of Spencer Percival, who became Prime Minister and won his place in the history books by being the only British Prime Minister to be assassinated in the House of Commons, which fate overtook him in 1809 on returning to London after a holiday fishing from his hotel gardens.

Edward Corbett, father of James Corbett, has recorded how, in the 1820s, following the disappearance of gas-tar from the water and the temporary return of the fish, he used to stand on New Bailey Bridge (later called Albert Bridge) and watch the shoals of gudgeon playing around the pillars of the bridge. So dense were the shoals, so numerous the fish rising to the flies, that the air was thick with swallows and house-martens. Local boys used to crack long whips through the air, throwing the lash so as to kill the birds on the wing.

Until very recently there has been no fishing in the Irwell within living memory; but the future holds a glimmer of promise, a hint that perhaps some of the efforts to clear pollution are succeeding. In the autumn of 1968 an engineer on a Danish ship in Manchester

Docks spotted a movement in the inky water. A keen angler, he quickly cast a line and hauled on board a full-grown pike. This tough and daring—and suicidal—specimen must have reached the docks via the Irwell itself. How he survived in those murky waters no one knows.

Late in 1971 the Bury Angling Society signed an agreement with Bury Corporation which gave the Society fishing rights along four miles of the river between Summerseat and the boundary of Radcliffe. The intention was to begin stocking experiments in the hope of breeding fish that will survive in the slowly-clearing waters.

Perhaps the angling days will indeed return, and fulfil the hope expressed in the last few lines of a poem written towards the end of the last century:

> And when the rainfalls pass from hill to sea
> Along a course from all things foul made free,
> We then may find our inky, stinky river
> A thing of beauty and a joy for ever.

By the mid-nineteenth century, steam packet boats were plying regularly along the Irwell and Mersey from Manchester and Salford, and in 1929 a correspondent writing in the *Manchester City News* under the name of "Burnageite" reminisced on such a journey taken for pleasure in 1866.

It was a great treat to my sister and me when my

mother took us occasionally on a fine summer's afternoon for a sail on the river. We descended from Blackfriars Bridge by some stone steps where the boat was waiting below. We took our seats. The boat started, and we were soon gliding past the backs of old houses and mills.

Gradually, the scenery on either side became less industrial, and instead of the grimy buildings there appeared green banks and trees, and cottages with gardens before them full of flowers. By this time the water was purer and the air clearer. On we went, past green fields where cows were feeding or lying lazily in the shade. Farmhouses were dotted here and there; ducks and geese swam near the banks. Occasionally we saw a man with rod and line fishing.

There were stopping places on the way where passengers could alight by a sort of platform which jutted out into the river. You could leave at Barton, Patricroft or Eccles. We were to leave near Barton and go up a country lane till we found a farmhouse or cottage where we had tea; after this we strolled about gathering wild flowers till the return of the boat about six or seven o'clock.

The mere joy of gliding along the river was not the only reason to take a packet boat in the nineteenth century. From the 1840s onward the boats would often be filled with pleasure-seekers on their way to Pomona Gardens, the only trace of which now is the name Pomona Dock near to where the gardens stood. The cost of travel to Pomona Gardens and all its wonders by either of the two packet boats named respectively *Punch* and *Judy,* was one penny from Victoria Bridge.

Pomona Gardens were rather like an early version of Belle Vue but with few animals, and covered a total of twenty-one acres of land, lying between the Irwell and the Chester Road, all devoted to pleasure. There were ballrooms, bright and gay with coloured paint, exotic carvings and mirrored pillars. There were artistic arbours and gentle paths winding among shrubberies and through small groves of apple trees. One of the marvels of the place was a clock tower standing fifty feet high with its face lit by gas at night.

On Mondays, Wednesdays and Saturdays—weather permitting—there were military bands, and every Whitsuntide a great carnival consisting of variety concerts, Negro minstrels, acrobatic performances, ballet—and Blondin. The famous tight-rope walker used to perform on a wire stretched across the open-air dance floor without a safety net. One of his tricks was to cook omelettes on a stove and throw them down to the people below.

Throughout the year there would be music festivals, cattle shows, brass band contests, athletic sports, firework displays, and rowing regattas on the river, in which Mark Addy sometimes took part. Political rallies were also held, attended on occasions by such well-known figures as Disraeli and Bright. In 1874 the TUC celebrated the first ten years of its existence by holding a great gathering attended by 80,000 workers.

Regattas have been held on the Irwell since 1842

when, on September 12, the first Manchester-Salford regatta was rowed on the straight stretch from Throstle Nest to the Regent Road Bridge. At least fifty pleasure boats were moored along the course, crowded with onlookers. The races included the "Irwell Stakes" for four-oared boats; the "Egerton Stakes" also for four oars; the "Sailing Match", the "Sculling Match" and "A Sweepstake".

The rowers were, according to Corbett, all working men. They swept past Pomona Gardens with Ordsall Hall on the opposite bank, past the chemical works, the sawmill, the Ordsall dye works and so to Regent Road Bridge.

The *Manchester Guardian* recorded that there was

> . . . bright sunshine and a pleasant breeze with many flags flying. The river banks were crowded with thousands of spectators, the favoured ones in the enclosure being entertained by the Salford Borough Band. The occasion was in every way worthy of the town and the improved state of the river.

The improvement, alas, was not to continue, and the regattas were abandoned in 1863. There was a revival for a few years from 1873 but the continuing deterioration of the river defeated the enthusiasts. Of all the rowing clubs the oldest survivor is the Agecroft Rowing Club founded in 1861 which, despite the condition of the river, celebrated its eighty-eighth regatta in June 1972.

During the same year, two crews of eights from Manchester and Salford Universities braved the murky waters and raced against each other, starting what is hoped may be an annual event. Manchester was the winner with an aggregate timing of 24.75 seconds faster than Salford. The race, against a background of time-stained factory and warehouse walls, so very different from that other and more classic contest on the Thames, was reported by veteran BBC commentator John Snagge.

The bows of the slim racing craft cut through the dark waters filthy with unmentionable rubbish, detergent and all the ingredients of a vicious chemical cocktail which needed first aid units to stand by in case anyone fell in. Fortunately this did not happen.

Watching from the river bank near Albert Bridge, facing a demolition site and a pumping station, it was possible with a great stretch of imagination to create in the mind a vision of a future Irwell on which oarsmen propel themselves through clean, clear waters, while spectators lounge on the grassy banks or stroll along riverside paths. Will it be like that when we celebrate the beginning of the twenty-first century? Or will it take fifty years? Or will it never be?

Another popular nineteenth-century sport by the Irwell was horse racing. This took place on the course established in 1847 within the great loop of the river in the Broughton district. The site was ideal because the river provided a natural barrier against intruders on three sides. Not everyone approved of horse racing and John Fitzgerald was one of its opponents. He came into ownership of the land and refused to renew the lease when it expired in 1867. Racing ceased then for more than thirty years until after Fitzgerald's death. Then in 1898 the Racecourse Company were able to buy back the land and racing began again in 1902.

In those days it was possible to walk round the loop by a riverside path, but today one needs a car to follow the Irwell. From Cromwell Road Bridge one travels along the still gracious, tree-lined Lower Broughton Road; something of an oasis, sheltered by trees and containing a picturesque mixture of houses in Edwardian pseudo-Gothic and pseudo-Elizabethan with black-and-white frontages, modern bungalows, stone terraced houses with bay windows, and a number of older three-storeyed dwellings which probably belonged to local cotton barons.

On maps the road is shown as continuing past the playing field established by Manchester Grammar School, past the football ground and on to Kersal Dale at the top of the loop. The road, however, makes a sudden swoop to the right along Hope Street. To stay parallel with the river one must continue on across the white line, ignoring Hope Street and following the "No entry except for access" sign.

At the top is the secluded Cliff Crescent, and here, along a narrow path to the left, is a fine view of the loop. Below lies a large factory, the only building encompassed by the river, and beyond the huge cluster of cliff dwellings that are Salford's modern high rise flats. The tip of the racecourse can also be seen.

The river continues past the Racecourse Hotel where it

is still possible to walk for some distance on a high banking between the river and the Littleton Playing Fields as far as Kersal Cell and the small boathouse owned by Agecroft Rowing Club.

Opposite the boathouse, on the Salford side of the river, is a municipal cemetery which contains one of the most unlikely of graves, that of Prince Peter Lobenguela, son of Lobenguela, King of the Matabele tribe of East Africa. In 1888 Cecil Rhodes, driven by his vision of an Africa coloured British red from Cape to Cairo, deceived Lobenguela and obtained control of his kingdom. When the chief died in 1894 his son was persuaded to sell himself to a circus owner who brought him to England to be exhibited as a specimen of the "noble savage". In the damp mists of Salford Prince Peter contracted tubercolosis and died. Now the son of a Zulu warrior rests by the Irwell.

13

A LIGHTER RIVER?

The completion of the Manchester Ship Canal in 1893 effectively canalized the Irwell by incorporating into it that section of the canal from the docks to beyond Brindley's aqueduct at Barton-on-Irwell, a place which logically ought now to be called Barton-on-Ship-Canal. It became obvious to everyone that this canalizing was going to make the effects of pollution much worse, especially during hot summers.

In 1891 the Mersey and Irwell Joint Committee was formed. This body concentrated its first efforts on compelling local authorities to provide sewage treatment facilities. Pressure was then brought to bear upon industrial concerns which were told to install the "best practical means" of preventing pollution.

The "best practical means" then available were normally little more than the installation of tanks for settlement and retention of solids. Whilst this must have helped in keeping solid matter out of the river, much of the oxygen-absorbing and polluting constituents were, and still are, in solution and continued to be discharged into the river.

In 1902 there were 445 manufacturers discharging effluent to the Mersey and Irwell within the Committee's jurisdiction. Today this figure is down to ninety. After the First World War the economic depression made it difficult to compel firms to finance better treatment plants, and until the passing of the Rivers (Prevention of Pollution) Act in 1951 the Committee was unable to prevent the emergence of a number of new industries such as the artificial silk and viscose industries which produced some very noxious effluents.

In 1939 the Joint Committee was superseded by yet another body, the Lancashire Rivers Board, and during the Second World War this Board realized that wartime conditions were causing a further deterioration in the Irwell. A major cause was the processing of straw by caustic soda boiling in the production of paper which saved the importation of pulp. Another cause of wartime deterioration was the kiering of gun-cotton at Rawtenstall and Radcliffe.

In 1951 the Board in its turn disappeared and was succeeded by the Mersey River Board under the River Board Act 1948. In 1965 this also went the way of all Boards and became the present Mersey and Weaver River Authority under the Water Resources Act 1963. This Board will disappear under another reorganization, for it is proposed that in April 1974 all River Authorities be merged into Regional Water Authorities which will include water supply undertakings and sewage disposal. The New Authority will in addition cover all land west of the Pennines from the Scottish border to Crewe.

Statistics provided by the Authority up to mid-1972 show that the normal flow of water at Adelphi Weir, Salford, is 120,000,000 gallons per day (g.p.d.) and included in this are 32,000,000 gallons of sewage from seven sewage works, plus 14,000,000 gallons of industrial effluent from twenty-one factories.

Formerly the river was badly polluted near to its source by effluent from textile printing works, but now it is fairly clean downstream to Rawtenstall, apart from where the upper reaches are discoloured by iron oxide originating in mine drainage. Sewage from Bacup, Rawtenstall and Haslingden, together with 5,000,000 g.p.d. of industrial effluent, is treated at a recently reconstructed sewage works at Ewood Bridge.

Limy Water which enters the river in Rawtenstall as compensation water from Clowbridge Reservoir is badly polluted by textile printing effluent.

The River Ogden, which joins the Irwell below Ewood Bridge, is polluted almost immediately by effluent from the bleaching of cotton linters. In Ramsbottom further pollution is caused by effluent from textile bleaching and by finishing from paper manufacture. Sewage from this area is treated at Ramsbottom Sewage Works at the rate of over 1,000,000 g.p.d.

In the Bury district further discharges are made into

the river and its tributaries from paper mills and textile finishing concerns. Sewage from the district is treated at Bury Sewage Works and runs at approximately 8,000,000 g.p.d.

The River Croal joining the Irwell at Prestolee, is an example of one stream which has been visibly improved. This was greatly helped by the closing down in recent years of many textile finishing works in the Bolton Area. There is also the new sewage works at Ringley Fold which deals with 15,000,000 g.p.d.

From Kearsley down towards Manchester the river improves despite discharges from another paper manufacturer and two chemical works. At Kearsley and Agecroft the power stations take in 70,000,000 gallons of river water every day for cooling purpose. This water is returned to the river unchanged in quality but 10°C warmer.

The River Roch rises at Summit between Todmorden and Littleborough and is seventeen miles in length. It joins the Irwell in Bury just downstream of Blackford Bridge. An average of just over 13,000,000 gallons of sewage from no less than eight sewage work is discharged into the Roch every day together with over 6,000,000 gallons of industrial effluent from twelve factories.

Above Littleborough the river is fairly clean but below the town there is serious pollution by effluent from a tannery and a chemical works. The poor quality of the effluent from Littleborough Sewage Works at 700,000 g.p.d. does not exactly help the situation. At the time of writing a scheme is under way for the construction of a trunk sewer which will carry the effluent to the Roch Mills Sewage Works. When this is completed it should be possible for the Roch in the Rochdale area to support fish life for the first time since 1835.

An important tributary is the River Beal which rises north of Oldham and enters the Roch at Smallbridge above Rochdale. The Beal is clean in the upper reaches but deteriorates badly where it receives Piethorn Brook at Newhey, polluted by effluent from textile, dyeing and finishing works. Below Rochdale town centre there is the River Spodden, badly polluted at Whitworth by textile finishing and printing effluent.

The Irk rises at Royton and after flowing through Middleton and Blackley enters the River Irwell by Victoria Station in Manchester. It is twelve miles long and has a normal flow of 13,000,000 g.p.d., 10,300,000 g.p.d. of sewage effluent from four sewage works discharge to the river together with 1,000,000 g.p.d. of trade effluent from two trade premises. Whilst still polluted it bears no comparison with former days when no fewer than fifty-five traders discharged effluent to this small river.

At Royton some pollution is caused by 350,000 g.p.d. of effluent from the Crompton U.D.C. Low Crompton Sewage Works, but the first serious pollution is from Royton Sewage Works (1,200,000 g.p.d.). A scheme to rebuild the Royton Works making provision for sewage at present treated at the Low Crompton Works is now in its final stages of preparation. In this area sewage pollution from defective storm sewage overflows occurs all too readily, and the Moston Brook suffers particularly in this respect.

The River Medlock springs into existence on the moors above Oldham and, after skirting that town, flows through the picturesque Daisy Nook at Failsworth and crosses the Manchester boundary at Clayton Bridge. At Knott Mill much of its flow is diverted into the Bridgewater Canal, the remainder passing through a culvert to the River Irwell. The Medlock is fifteen miles long and has a normal flow of 6,000,000 g.p.d. About 1,900,000 g.p.d. of sewage effluent from three sewage works is discharged into the river together with various small but highly polluting discharges of piggery effluent from many farms in the Woodhouses area. Attempts are being made to use as much as possible of this effluent as fertilizer.

Pollution is a popular theme today, often over-dramatized by the media, but that is better than having the problem understated. In May 1972, Manchester University announced the inauguration of a new Master of Science degree in Pollution and Environmental Research. The first twelve students were due to start a one-year course in the following October. In December 1971, the Government made it known that £1,300,000,000 was due to be made available to clear the polluted rivers of Britain during the next few years. This sum represents an increase of about 50 per cent in real terms over capital expenditure on water supply and sewage disposal schemes, and the area covered by the Mersey and Weaver River Authority should benefit by about 10 per cent of the whole.

Sir William Mather, Chairman of the Civic Trust for the North-West, speaking of the £1,300,000,000, has said that "We have a bigger pollution problem in the North-West than any similar area in the world. We should have a share related to the problem and not to any territorial area".

The task of clearing up the mess of two centuries is going to be slow and unspectacular, even with so much money. The Authority has to practise the infinitely tedious and time-consuming business of trying to "persuade" and "educate" the numerous firms and local authorities to find ways of consuming their waste products. There is no financial incentive for any of them to do so—rather the opposite, for pollution prevention costs money. It brings no reward other than that of making a pleasanter environment for our brief lives on this planet. It helps us to act as responsible custodians instead of indifferent despoilers of our earth. It helps us to atone for the crimes against the environment committed in the past—high principles to introduce at a shareholders' meeting!

There is a marked difference in the approach made to the problems by certain other countries for whom the drip-drip slowness of English gradualism has no appeal. In Rome, two prominent industrialists were sent to prison in May 1972, charged with polluting the Tiber with waste from their factories. The warrants for their arrest were signed by a Rome magistrate who had been conducting an enquiry into river pollution. Such stern treatment from the magistrates of Manchester and Salford would doubtless bring some agitated letters to *The Guardian* from the boardrooms along the Irwell.

A hopeful sign was the judgement handed down in May 1972 by the House of Lords in the case of an appeal by a Radcliffe firm against a conviction for pollution. The company had allowed polluted water to enter the Irwell but not knowingly or negligently. The Lords, however, judged that "Unless the prosecution could discharge the often impossible task of proving that pollution was caused intentionally or negligently, a great deal of pollution would go unpunished". The appeal was dismissed.

In the late nineteenth century Joseph Anthony wrote this poem:

> Whoe'er hath seen dark Irwell's tide,
> Its sombre look and sullen glide,
> Would never deem that it, I ween,
> Had ever brighter, gayer been.
> When Irwell rolled by feudal tower,
> By shady grove, and fairy bower,
> When on her banks so oft was borne
> Sweet music of the hunter's horn.
> Forests are here, but not of trees;
> Forests are here, the homes of men,
> Mancunians sons are as the leaves,
> Which bloomed upon the forest then.

Curiously enough, even in the present century, there have been some for whom the Irwell even in its present state holds a certain charm. The late F. A. Bruton who wrote *A Short History of Manchester and Salford* in 1927 (reprinted in 1970) gives us this quotation from an earlier writer whose name is not revealed:

> Loyal Manchester men, homing from Florence, San Francisco or Constantinople, will pause entranced on leaving the station, to lean over the bridge, and come into their own again. Below, on the torpid stream, refuse swirls draw sheeny curvilinear grainings, parodies of a rainbow's Palette, on a chocolate ground; late at night the quiet lifts in relief the still, small multitudinous plop of bubbles rising and breaking, a million infinitesimal belches. Day or night, as at the passing of Cleopatra's barge,
>
> "A faint, invisible perfume hits the sense
> Of the adjacent wharves",
>
> wharves partly, factories mostly, springing their sixty feet of sheer out of the viscous fluid, their walls bored here and there with pipes of all calibres, some spitting fitful white rods of steam; from others, their nozzles flush with the bricks, all the waste filths of industry, bilges and rinsings and dirtgorged greases, suppurate slowly and cake on the walls coat upon coat. You might say, not having love, a "Venice in Hell"; but what are Thames and Tiber, Abana and Pharphar, to

this Jordan, for this Israel? Here they feel clean and blunt again; "jannock" they call it.

The politically-minded blame the capitalist system for this spoliation of our environment; but in fact it is not any "system" that is the cause. A recent report in a Soviet magazine indicates that communism has been just as heedless about its environment. Caviar is said to be about to become an even greater rarity because the industrial filth poured into the Volga and the Caspian is killing off the sturgeon.

The simple fact is that man has never regarded himself as the custodian of the planet earth, but has looked upon it as a rich storehouse of treasures put there by a benevolent creator for him to loot—and the animal kingdom for him to exploit.

In the course of looting and exploiting, man, the parasite species, finds himself with a growing volume of rubbish to throw away, and seems to regard the rivers and oceans as having been created for the purpose of carrying away such rubbish.

Only in recent years have we begun to realize that the treasurehouse is not inexhaustible, and the capacity of the waterways to absorb waste is not infinite.

Several generations have dreamed of a clean and pure Irwell, and we in the 1970s may have the last chance to achieve this.

If we are luckier than seems likely, by the end of the decade there could be a gracious tree-lined promenade along the Crescent in Salford, green banks and peaceful paths by Chetham's College, punts and rowing boats gliding leisurely on Sunday afternoons by Ordsall Hall; and in a hundred places people fishing for salmon and gudgeon.

Flow sweetly, Irwell, as you did before the machines came.

BIBLIOGRAPHY

Ashmore, Owen, *Industrial Archaeology of Lancashire.* David & Charles, 1969.

Aspin, C., *Lancashire, the First Industrial Society.* Helmshore Local History Society, 1969.

Axon, W. E. A., *Annals of Manchester,* John Heywood.

Banks, Mrs Linnæus, *The Manchester Man.* John Sherratt and Son Ltd., reprinted 1970.

Bruton, F. A., *A Short History of Manchester and Salford.* Sherratt & Hughes, 1927; reprinted by S. R. Publishers Ltd., 1970.

Corbett, J., *The River Irwell.* Abel Heywood, 1907.

Croston, James, *Nooks and Corners of Lancashire and Cheshire.* John Heywood, 1882.

Credland, W. R., *Days Out.* Printed for the author by T. Sowler & Sons Ltd., 1898.

Davies, G. E. & A. R., *The River Irwell and its Tributaries.* John Heywood, 1890.

Falk, Bernard, *The Bridgewater Millions.* Hutchinson, 1942.

Faucher, Leon, *Manchester in* 1844. Abel Heywood.

Gaskell, Peter, *The Manufacturing Population of England*. Baldwin & Craddock, 1833.

Hayes, Louis M., *Reminiscences of Manchester*. Sherratt & Hughes, 1905.

Hewitt, Margaret, *Wives and Mothers in Victorian Industry*. Rockliffe, 1958.

Kay, J. Phillips, *Moral and Physical Condition of the Working Classes*. First published 1832; reprinted, E. J. Morten, 1969.

Robinson, W., *The Mersey and Irwell*. B. Taylor & Co., 1888.

Talon, Henri, *John Byrom*. Rockliffe, 1950.

Taylor, W. Cooke, *Notes of a Tour in the Manufacturing Districts of Lancashire*. Frank Cass Co. Ltd., 1842; reprinted 1970.

Watts, John, *Facts of the Cotton Famine*. Frank Cass Co. Ltd., 1866; reprinted 1968.

Ward, J. T., *The Factory System*. David & Charles; reprinted 1968.

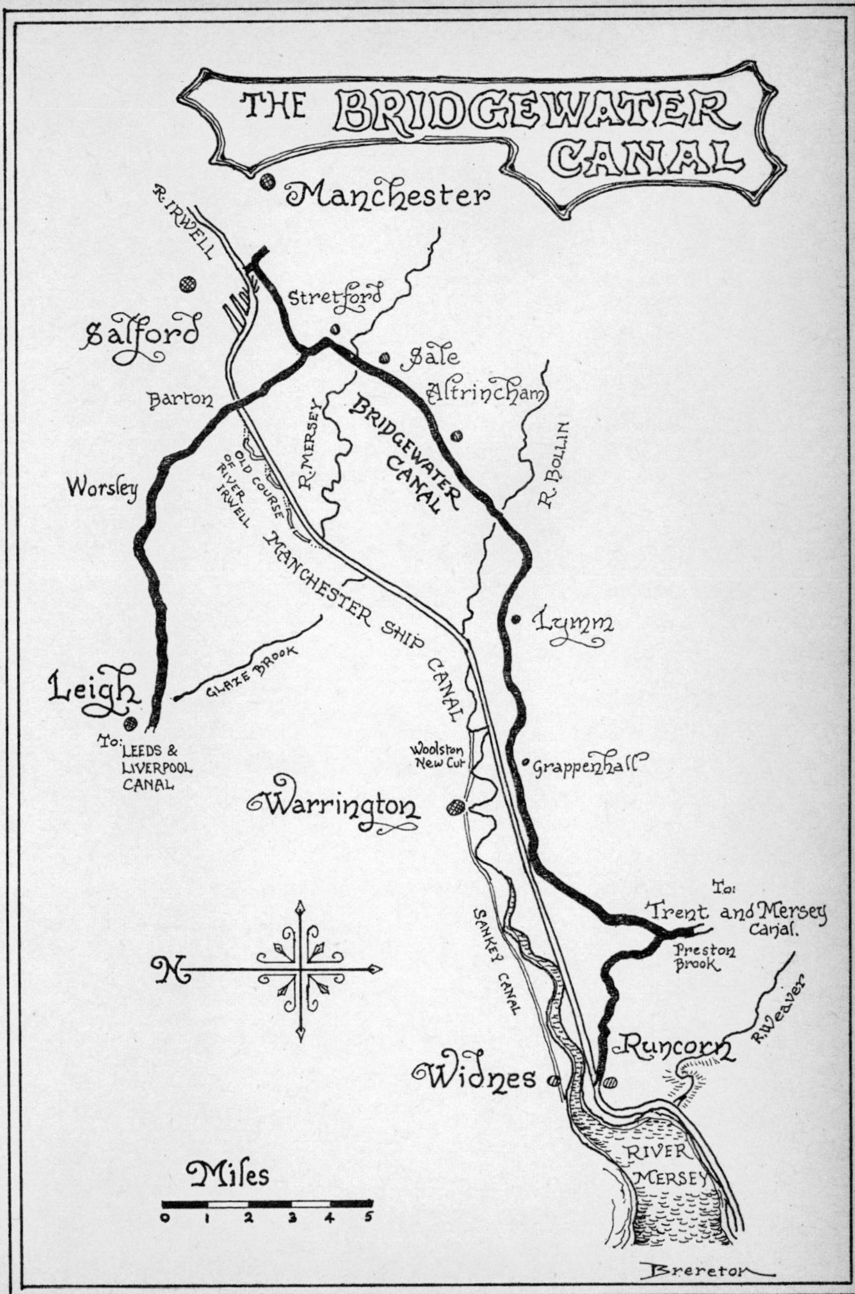
THE BRIDGEWATER CANAL
Manchester
R. IRWELL
Salford
Stretford
Sale
Altrincham
Barton
Worsley
R. MERSEY
BRIDGEWATER CANAL
OLD COURSE OF RIVER IRWELL
R. BOLLIN
MANCHESTER SHIP CANAL
Lymm
GLAZE BROOK
Leigh
To: LEEDS & LIVERPOOL CANAL
Woolston New Cut
Grappenhall
Warrington
To: Trent and Mersey Canal.
Preston Brook
SANKEY CANAL
R. Weaver
N
Runcorn
Widnes
RIVER MERSEY
Miles
0 1 2 3 4 5
Brereton

RIVER IRWELL
and
Tributaries
Deerplay Moor
Bacup
Rochdale
Waterfoot
Rossendale Valley
RIVER ROCH
Scout Moor
Rawtenstall
Ramsbottom
Summerseat
RIVER IRWELL
Holcombe Moor
BRADSHAW BROOK
EAGLEY BROOK
ASTLEY BROOK
Turton Moor
Smithills Moor

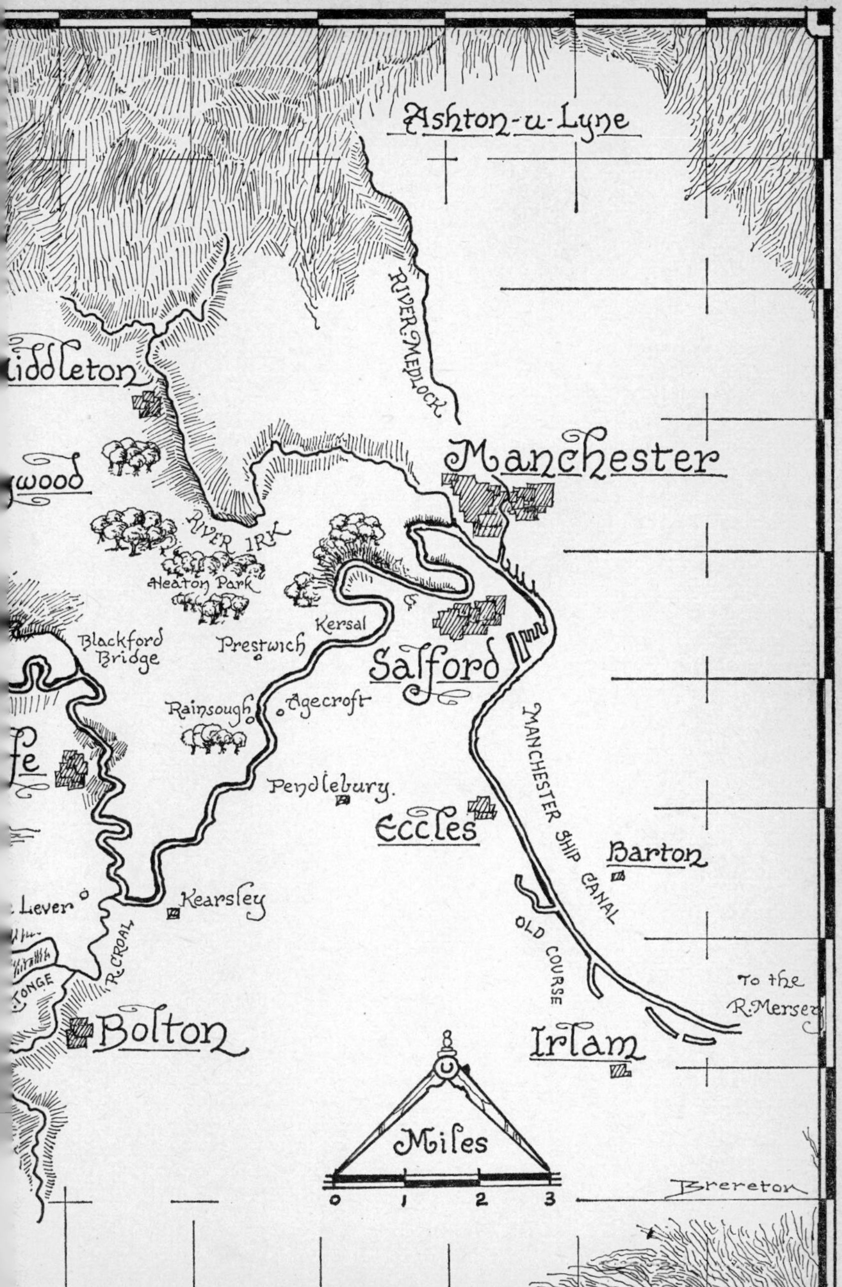

Ashton-u-Lyne
River Medlock
Middleton
Manchester
River Irk
Heaton Park
Kersal
Prestwich
Blackford Bridge
Salford
Rainsough
Agecroft
Pendlebury.
Eccles
Manchester Ship Canal
Barton
Lever
Kearsley
R. Croal
Tonge
Old Course
To the R. Mersey
Bolton
Irlam
Miles
0
1
2
3
Brereton

INDEX

Index

Index

Index